D1570247

Well Then There Now

Well Then There Now

Juliana Spahr

A Black Sparrow Book

David R. Godine · *Publisher*

Boston

This is
A Black Sparrow Book
published in 2011 by
David R. Godine • Publisher
Post Office Box 450
Jaffrey, New Hampshire 03452
www.blacksparrowbooks.com

Book design by Jacqueline Thaw.

The Black Sparrow pressmark is by Julian Waters.

Library of Congress Cataloging-in-Publication Data

Spahr, Juliana.
  Well then there now / Juliana Spahr.
     p. cm.
  "A Black Sparrow book."
  ISBN 978-1-57423-217-2 (pbk.)
  I. Title.
  PS3569.P3356W455 2011
  811'.54—dc22
                        2010034171

First Edition, Second Printing
Printed in the United States

CONTENTS

ACKNOWLEDGEMENTS AND OTHER INFORMATION

"Some of We and the Land That Was Never Ours," "Dole Street,"
"2199 Kalia Road," "Unnamed Dragonfly Species," and "Gentle
Now, Don't Add to Heartache" were all self-published under the
Subpoetics, Self-Publish or Perish initiative.

"Some of We and the Land That Was Never Ours" was written at
3029 Lowrey Avenue, Honolulu, Hawai'i 96822. It was published in
the *Chicago Review* and then reprinted in *Best American
Poems of 2001*.

"Sonnets" was written at 3029 Lowrey Avenue, Honolulu,
Hawai'i 96822. Some of "Sonnets" was originally published in
Conjunctions under the title "Blood Sonnets." The sonnet that
begins "We arrived" was originally published in *Tinfish*.

"Dole Street" was written at 2955 Dole Street, Honolulu, Hawai'i
96822. Excerpts were previously published in *Bombay Gin* and in
Mixed Blood.

"Things of Each Possible Relation Hashing Against One Another"
was written at 2955 Dole Street, Honolulu, Hawai'i 96822 and at
435 Clermont Avenue, Brooklyn, New York 12238. It was originally
published as a chapbook by Palm Press. Sections of these poems
previously appeared in *Pom2*, *PoEP*, and *The Ampersand*.

"Unnamed Dragonfly Species" was written at 435 Clermont
Avenue, Brooklyn, New York 12238. It was originally written for
a reading in the Drawing Center Series (curated by Lytle Shaw)
held during the "Ellsworth Kelly Tablet: 1949 – 1973" exhibit at the
Drawing Center in New York City. Selections from it were published
in *The Poker* and in *Ecopoetics*. The list of endangered, threatened

and special concern plant, fish, and wildlife species of New York
State is from the New York State Department of Environmental
Conservation, www.dec.state.ny.us/website/dfwmr/wildlife/
endspec/etsclist.html.

"2199 Kalia Road" was written at 3061 Pualei Circle, Honolulu,
Hawai'i 96815. It was originally written for the website *Historic
Waikīkī* at downwindproductions.com.

"Gentle Now, Don't Add to Heartache" was written at 5000
MacArthur Boulevard, Oakland, California 94613. It was originally
published in *Tarpaulin Sky*. While this poem was written in Oakland,
California, it is about Chillicothe, Ohio. It owes a number of debts:
to a writing workshop at Goddard College in the winter residency of
2004, to a hypnotherapy session with Michelle Ritterman,
to *A Guide to Ohio Streams* (published by the Ohio Chapter of the
American Fisheries Society), to *The Path of the Rainbow: The Book of
Indian Poems* (edited by George W. Cronyn), to Gail Holst-Warhaft's
Dangerous Voices: Women's Laments and Greek Literature (thanks to
Allison Cobb for reference to this book). The "gentle now" was stolen
from Ibn 'Arabī's "Gentle Now, Doves" as translated by Michael
A. Sells (collected in *Stations of Desire: Love Elegies from Ibn 'Arabī
and New Poems*).

"The Incinerator" was written at 2127 Blake Street, Berkeley,
California 94704. It was originally published in *Lana Turner:
A Journal of Poetry and Opinion*. Hannah Weiner's "Radcliffe and
Guatemalan Women" is in *Open House* (Kenning Editions, 2006).

I've left Hawaiian words as they were in original publications.
Thanks everyone. Thanks Jackie. Thanks especially also BL and CW.
Thanks Mills Faculty Development grant.

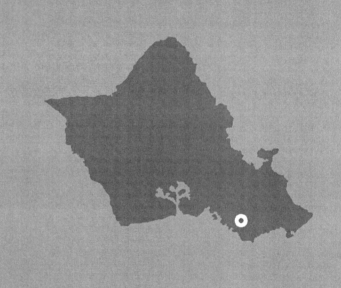

N **21°** 18' 28" W **157°** 48' 28"

Some of We
and the Land That Was
Never Ours

Steinim
with the
world
grape
except we
goes
beyond

human

(someday
poets
eve)

We are all. We of all the small ones are. We are all. We of all the small ones are. We are in this world. We are in this world. We are together. We are together. And some of we are eating grapes. Some of we are all eating grapes. Some of we are all eating. We are all in this world today. Some of we are eating grapes today in this world. And some of we let ourselves eat grapes. In the eating of grapes. We of all the small ones are what eats grapes. In the world of grapes. Eating grapes. We of all the small ones are what eats. Some of we are all together in the grapes. We of all the small ones are today in this world. In this world. By eating grapes. To eat grapes. Some of we let ourselves eat grapes today in this world. Some of we let ourselves be all together in the grapes. In the world of the grapes. In this world. In the grapes. In the grapes. In taste. In the taste. In fermentation. In fermentation. In wine. Out of the wine. In fresh tight skin. In the fresh tight skin. In seed. Out of seed. In moisture. In moisture. In today. In today. We are all in this world together. We of all the small ones are together in this world. In the we are all together. In we let ourselves be all together. Some of we are eating. Some of we let ourselves eat. Some of we are all together eating grapes. Some of we let ourselves be all the grapes to be eaten together. In this place. In this place. In the eating. While eating. In the grapes some of we are all eating. In all the undeniable grapes of we let us leave itself let ourselves be what eats. In the eating of grapes. By eating grapes. We are all today. We of all the small ones are today. The grapes in the eating. In the we are. In the are. In the grapes are. Eating grapes. In the we the world. In the together. Some of we are all in this world together eating grapes.

Some of we and the land that was never ours while we were the land's. Started from us and of the ground which was never with we while we were the ground. Some of we wore the land. Some of we carried the ground. Some of we planted grapes. We ate the sheets of the ground. But we were made by the ground, by the grapes. Grapes of the ground. Some of we planted grapes. Green of the ground. Some of we were to settle. Some of we were to arrange. And the land was never ours. And the ground was never with us. And yet we were made by the land, by the grapes. We were eating the leaves of the land. The grapes of the land. The green of the land. The leaves. Sheets. And we were the land's because we were eating and the land let some of us eat. And we were the ground because we eat and the ground let some among us eat. And yet the land was never some of ours. But the ground was never sure with us. Is never some of ours. Be never certain with us. Never will be rightly some of ours. Be correctly never certain with us. Never to be owned. Never to be had. And the land's green is the land's owning of us. And the green of the ground is the possession of the ground of us.

The land is some of us holding out our hand and sparrows are pecking at it eating. The ground is among us giving our hand and the sparrows picotent with it eating. We are all in this world, this world of hands and grain, together. We all the small ones are in this world, this world of the hands and grain, together. Some of us are sparrows pecking at our hand. Some among us are sparrows picotant with our hand. Flying then nesting on our finger. With then control the hardware on our finger. Sparrows are pecking at our hand, pecking at our grain, at our hand, at our grain, at our hand. The sparrows picotent with our hand, picotant with our grain, our hand, our grain, our hand. We are all in this world with sparrows. We all the small ones are in this world with sparrows. With pecking. With the picoter. We are in this hand, in this pecking. We are in this hand, in this picoter. We are all. We all the small ones are. Some of we are pecking back. Some of we left ourselves picotons behind. We are pecking at our hand. We picotons with our hand. We are wanting to be full with grain. We want to be full with the grain. And then to be eating grapes. And to eat grapes then. Some of we are flying at our hand, flying at our hand. Some of we let ourselves fly to our hand, rollings up with our hand. Some of we are pecking at our hand of flying. Some of we left ourselves picotons with our hand of the flight. We are all in this world together, flying pecking. We all the small ones are together in this world, controlling the picoter. Down on the ground. With bottom on the ground. Then again, flying, pecking. The other side, to fly, picotant.

—

13

What it means to settle. What means it arrangement. To we are all in this world together. We all the small ones are together in this world. To eat the grapes and not to plant the seed. To eat the grapes and not to plant seed. To hold on too tight. To be too strongly held in the function. To change. To change. To make the change. To make the change. To change the land. To change the ground. To throw out the seed. To throw out of seed. To we are all in this world together yet still some of we are eating grapes, others pecking at the hand. We all the small ones are together in this world always however that some of us eat grapes, others which picotent with the hand. How to move. How to move. How to move from settle on top to inside. How to move stabilization on the top inside. To embrace, to not settle. To embrace, not to arrange. To speak. To speak. To spoke. With the spoke. To poke away at what it is that is wrong in this world we are all in together. To push far what is with it is incorrect in this world which all the small ones are us in the unit.

Note: *We were tourists in France. There were long lines. My mother waited in them. I sat outside and took notes. In the park, someone was singing we are all in this world together. There were some grapes. Someone was feeding sparrows, making them perch on the thumb and eat out of the hand if they wanted any food. The sparrows preferred to eat on the ground. I was thinking about a story I had heard about a French grandfather who left early in my father's life, moved to Canada, and died by falling off a horse. I thought about the vines that grew in France, then came as cuttings to California, then went back to France after a blight. I thought about who owned what. And divisions. And songs sung in bars. And inaugural poems. I was just trying to figure out this day. I came home and used a translation machine to push my notes back and forth between French and English until a different sort of English came out: this poem.*

—

15

N **21°** 18' 28" W **157°** 48' 28"

Sonnets

We arrived.

We arrived by air, by 747 and DC10 and L1011.

We arrived over the islands and we saw the green of them
    out the window.

We arrived and then walked into this green.

Things were different.

The air was moist and things were different.

Plants grew into and on top of and around each other and things
    were different.

The arrival of those before us made things different.

We tried not to notice but as we arrived we became a part of arriving
    and making different.

We grew into it but with complicities and assumptions
    and languages

and kiawe and koa haole and mongooses.

With these things we kicked out certain other things whether we
    meant to or not.

Asking what this means matters.

And the answer also matters.

—

19

white blood cells at 4.2 thousand per cubic millimeter
red blood cells at 3.88 million per cubic millimeter
hemoglobin at 14.1 grams per decaliter
hematocrit at 42.6 %

mean corpuscular volume at 109.6 fluid liquid
mean corpuscular hemoglobin at 36.3 picograms per cell
mean corpuscular hemoglobin concentration at 33.1 %
red blood cell distribution width at 13. 5 %

platelets at 216 thousand per cubic millimeter
mean platlet volume at 7.8 fluid liquid
granulocyte percent at 62.4
lymphocyte percent at 27.0

monocyte percent at 8.6
eosinophil percent at 1.4

As intricate system we are.

We with all with our complexities.

We with all our identifications.

We with all our homes and our irregularities live.

We are full of thought and we live.

We live with things several.

We are full of thought and we are different.

For which things so several.

—

21

The catalogue of the life span, the operation, and the animal.

The catalogue of force and animal life.

The catalogue of the extension of life, the operation, and the animal.

The catalogue of the extension of the execution of life and the animal.

Togetherness of the lesson and the splitting.

Togetherness of the lesson and to duplicate one's self.

basophil percent at 0.6

granulocyte absolute at 2.6 thousand per cubic millimeter

lymphocyte absolute at 1.1 %

monocyte absolute at 0.4 %

eosinophil absolute at 0.1 %

basophil absolute at 0.0 thousand per cubic millimeter

alanine amino tranferafe serum at 21 units per liter

cholesterol at 171 milligrams per decaliter

alkaline phosphatase at 46 units per liter

gamma-glutamyl transpeptidase at 22 units per liter

bilirubin total at 0.5 milligrams per decaliter

high density lipoprotein at 52 milligrams per decaliter

low density lipoprotein at 124 milligrams per decaliter

cholesterol/high density lipoprotein at 3.6 risk

Things should be said more largely than the personal way.

Things are larger than the personal way of telling.

Intimate confession is a project.

Confession's structured plan of percents and regulations.

When the amounts of blood are considered.

When the strength, the quantities, of blood are regarded.

When blood is thought as meaning.

An intimate confession.

—

23

Blood is a force, a house.

And the difference between those that took and those that remained.

As the qualities of blood are considered remains undocumentable.

As the quantities of blood are considered remains unquantifiable.

For we are located with some and not with others for this is intimate.

We are situated with some and not with one against confession.

time drawn at 1819
absolute lymphocyte at 1134 cubic millimeter
cd3 % (total t) at 88
cd3 at 1004 cubic millimeter

cd4 % (helper) at 39.9
cd4 at 452 cubic millimeter
cd8 % (supres) at 46.6
cd8 at 528 cubic millimeter

cd4/cd8 ration at 0.9
sodium at 137 milliequivalents per liter
potassium at 4.6 milliequivalents per liter
chloride at 98 milliequivalents per liter

carbon dixoide at 26 milliequivalents per liter
blood urea nitrogen at 17 milligrams per decaliter

A catalogue of the individual and a catalogue of us with all.

A catalogue of full of thought.

A house where we with all our complexities lie.

A catalogue of blood.

A catalogue of us with all our complexities.

A catalogue of how we are all full of thought and connection.

The house where we are from and the house where we live.

All things to be said more largely than the personal way.

—
25

There is in this the thought of home.

Those who had a home.

Those who have a right to a home.

And there is those who took and those who stayed in the taking.

The house of difference when we look.

The house of norms and abnormalities and their percentages.

glucose at 111 milligrams per decaliter
creatinine at 0.9 milligrams per decaliter
calcium at 9.4 milligrams per decaliter
total protein at 7.1 grams per decaliter

albumin at 4.5 grams per decaliter
lactic dehydrogenase at 171 international units per liter
aspartate amino tranferafe serum at 25 international units per liter
rapid plasma reagin at nonreactive

rapid plasma reagin titer at 1:2
flourescent treponemal antibody, absorbed at nonreactive
hepatitis b surface antigen at negative
hepatitis b surface antibody at negative

hepatitis c antibody at negative
gonnococcal/chlamydia at negative

Who of comparison.

Who of analogy.

Who of empathy.

Who of structural alignment.

Who authorizes so one is not what individual one says one is.

Who authorizes so one is not single.

Who empowers so one is not alone.

Who is expert of confession.

Who one is situated with and not with others.

Who one lies with and not with others.

Who is characterized how by some and not by others.

Who is various.

For who is located with some and not with stillness.

For who is asking and then listening.

—

27

We arrived and everything was interconnected:
as twining green maile shrub,
as huehue haole.
Our response was to uproot and to bunker.

We arrived and the rain soaked us regularly
as it soaked others and fed rivulets and streams.
It was gentle and warm
but still we built and we bunkered.

This growing and this flowing into all around us confused us.
We didn't know the right and the wrong.
We couldn't tell where we began and where we ended with the land
    and with the others,
where we loved and where we didn't and where we weren't even
    though we longed.

And because we could not figure it out bunkering was a way for us
    to claim what wasn't really ours, what could never really be
    ours and it gave us a power we otherwise would not have had
    and we believed that this made the place ours.
But because we were bunkered, the place was never ours, could
    never really be ours, because we were bunkered from what
    mattered, growing and flowing into, and because we could not
    begin to understand that this place was not ours until we
    grew and flowed into something other than what we were we
    continued to make things worse for this place of growing
    and flowing into even while some of us came to love it and let
    it grow in our own hearts, flow in our own blood.

N **21°** 17' 26.52" W **157°** 48' 37.4436"

Dole Street

one

I live and I work on Dole Street. So I walk up and down Dole Street.

Dole Street is named after Sanford B. Dole who was born in Honolulu in 1844. He was president of the Provisional Government (1893–1894) and the Republic of Hawai'i (1895–1898), and first governor of the Territory of Hawai'i (1898–1903).

When I first moved to Dole Street, I thought that it was named after the Dole of pineapples. But that was a relative, James Dole. James got the land for his pineapples from Sanford's governments. Sanford Dole was an annexationist. He felt that Hawaiians should not be allowed to vote in the new democratic government that he helped establish: "I believe it is exceedingly necessary to keep out of politics this class of people, irresponsible people I mean."

Dole also wrote satirical plays about the current events of his time. They tend to mock King Kalākaua. They call the King things like Emperor Skyhigh. Dole and friends also called Kalākaua the "Merry Monarch" because he liked hula and mele.

Dole Street is two lanes wide near the university. But between Wilder and Punahou, it is often only one lane wide and when two cars meet, one must pull off to the side to let the other car pass. Dole runs in the 'Ewa and Diamond Head direction (which is more west and east than anything else).

As I am always walking on Dole Street, I am always thinking about Dole Street.

two

The walk along Dole Street is often boring and hot.

Last year I was given a very small camera that I could keep in my backpack. I started taking pictures of stickers people put on their cars as I walked to and from work. Most of the stickers that I saw had to do with girls, Hawai'i, and surfing.

Companies like Local Motion and Roxy that sell surf products especially like to use this trinity of girls, Hawai'i, and surfing to advertise their brands. These companies sell Hawai'i as they sell surfing gear and accessories. They like images of girls in bikinis with hibiscus behind their ears. Or images of girls surfing in grass skirts. They are about Hawai'i in the way that Gidget is about Hawai'i (continental import that sells Hawai'i to the continent and then it ricochets back to Hawai'i). It is said that Roxy does not make large size clothing because they do not want their brand name on big girls.

The back windows of trucks are popular places to put stickers. Giant girls in bathing suits with provocative poses often go here. Or sometimes a big huge fish skeleton that advertises a surf brand.

Often cars pile up references. There might be a mechanized hula doll, one of those whose hips shake when turned on, on the dashboard. Then a sticker on the back window of a hula girl with exaggerated breasts wearing only a lei and a grass skirt and posing like a '50s pin-up girl. Beside this, a statement of faith in the power of hooters. You can buy the hula doll at any of the thousands of ABC stores in Waikīkī. She comes with a pink or green skirt that is made out of plastic and she has really big hips. The ABC offers a discount if you buy five or more to take home as gifts. It seems that girls on cars help boys in their twenties. The west is best when girls go Pacific such cars say.

—
35

Not all stickers on cars are only about male desire. Some might be about self-identity (Kaua'i girl) as much as they might be about desire (Kaua'i girls!). Kaua'i Boys is also a band. Every island except

O'ahu seems to have its own stickers. There is one for Kaua'i
that says "Garden Island Brotherhood." There are also stickers
that go across the front of the windshield and that say
something like "Molokainian" or "Tongan" or "Tahiti To'a" in 4"

letters. There are stickers that say "Hawaii Built" or "Maui Built"
or "Maui Built Hawaiian."

Once I noticed that someone had altered their license plate
and had taped the words "PONO N KAINAHE" over the rainbow
that decorates the license plate. I know that "pono" has a lot of
meanings such as goodness or righteousness or equity or proper
respectfulness. It is in the state motto and it is often pointed out
that the state doesn't even uphold its own motto. Pono is also a
band. But I don't know what "kainahe" means except that it can be
used as a woman's name. I can't tell if this is a slogan of some sort
or just another sign of desire between men and women.

three

Where these cars are parked, and before the university proper
begins, Dole Street has a huge cliff on its mauka side. I do not know
who owns this land. There are trails along the cliff and dirt bikers
ride down them and rush out into traffic if they don't brake quickly.

Homeless people climb up the paths to a series of caves where they sometimes spend the night.

After the parking ends, there is a bee's nest tucked into a small opening in the side of the cliff. The bees have made so much hive that it is spilling out, exposed to the sun. Eventually some of them will swarm.

In one spot near the bees, someone has spray painted "kuʻe," or resistance, along the sheer rock.

After the cliff is Mānoa Stream. Dole Street passes over it. The stream travels from the back of the valley where it tends to rain more. The growth next to the stream is rich and the trees from the stream shade the road. When I am walking to work, the shade is always a relief and I often stop to look at what is growing in the stream. The other day I noticed these trees: wiliwili, kukui, ʻōhiʻa lehua, African tulip tree, and koa haole. Kalo grows along the banks. I don't know if the kalo was planted there by humans or if it was dropped there by an animal. There is a loʻi nearby, a terrace for growing dryland kalo, that is run by the Center for Hawaiian Studies, one of few departments at the university that actively educates students in ongoing resistance to colonialism. The stream is diverted so that it circulates through the loʻi constantly bringing in fresh water.

After the stream along Dole Street are two public art projects. One is called "Gate of Hope" and it was made by Alexander Liberman in 1972. It was commissioned by the state and paid for by a fund that was made by a law that required one percent of construction appropriations be used for art. This fund was flush while the island was building in the 1970s and 1980s but has been more or less worthless in the recession that has defined the state since the 1990s. The sculpture is some orange tubes arranged in a modern art-like pattern. "Gate of Hope" has a little sign in front of it that says that it refers to engineering principles that allow people to build complex structures. The joke though is that the sculpture looks like a giant hand giving the finger to Waikīkī off in the distance.

The other is called "Chance Meeting" and it is by George Segal. It was also commissioned by the state. It is a sculpture of three people standing around talking in high realist fashion. These people look haole in feature, are very short at around 5' tall maximum, are older, and are dressed for late fall on the east coast. Next to these people is a complicated sign that says "mauka" and points to the mountains, that says "makai" and points to the sea, that says "'Ewa" and points 'Ewa, that says "Koko Head" and points Koko Head. Despite this sign, the sculpture is a classic example of inapplicable public art and inattentiveness to the local. It often makes me laugh to think of these people conversing confusedly in their raincoats in the hot sun about the terms mauka and makai, terms that tourists learn on their first day on the island. In my more generous moments, I like to read this sculpture as an example of the clash between the local and the continental that so defines the university. An ironic comment of sorts. I see my often hot, confused, and regularly inapplicably dressed self among the figures. But the term "chance meeting" bugs me. To me, the sculpture is only interesting if it, like Dole Street, speaks of how three haoles never meet by chance in Hawai'i. Its representation is so specific, and so not representational of life in Hawai'i, that it does not seem neutral, or chance, at all. Maybe another way to read the sculpture would be as the lie of realism. Often people drape leis over the necks of the figures or put traffic cones on top of their heads as hats.

PUNAHOU
o

MARY KNOLL
o

UNIVERSITY OF HAWAI'I
o

ST. LOUIS
o

four

I like the stickers of Dole Street mainly because they tell of connections between humans and humans or between humans and the land and all the lovely possibilities and sad humiliations of these connections. But Dole Street is a road and it connects things in other ways. There are three private schools and one research university, the only one in the state, on Dole Street. St. Louis, a Catholic high school is at one end (near where I live). Dole passes through the middle of the University of Hawai'i, Mānoa, where I work and why I live in Hawai'i. At its other end is Mary Knoll, another private school. And across the street from Mary Knoll, but not on Dole, is Punahou, an elite private high school. Punahou was founded by missionaries for their children and the children of ali'i. After annexation, it became notorious as the haole school, attended mainly by the children of settlers who wanted to get their kids out of the multi-ethnic, pidgin speaking public schools. The school casts a large shadow in the psychic imagination of the state. It tends to be mentioned with reverence or hate, rarely with anything else. Many politicians attend it, go away to college on the continent, then come back to run the state.

    I do not want to make too much of these connections or to suggest that it extends to the level of conspiracy. It is rather more mundane. Houses, after all, are in between the schools. Parts of Dole

Street are middle class and parts are more working class and people of many different races and ethnicities and concerns live on it.

But the names of streets and buildings and schools and parks always tell a history. And in this sense, Dole Street is another poem about bad history. In Hawai'i, an official street name that is a haole name means the street is one of the older ones, named in the middle years of the 19th century most likely, and it usually is named after some annexation or post-annexation figure. Pukui, Elbert, and Mookini who wrote Place Names of Hawaii—this book made this essay possible—notice that street names are limited to these categories: discoverers, missionaries, business men, educators, politicians, and military officers. Dole Street is intersected by a whole series of streets named after less important haoles who are less than honorable and who would have known one another by forces other than chance. It is this cluster of haole names that interests me. 86% of place names in Hawai'i are Hawaiian (again Pukui, Elbert, and Mookini). Only four of the streets that intersect Dole have Hawaiian names. There is Punahou of course. But for many, the private school occupies the name. The other streets that intersect Dole with Hawaiian names are Kānewai, water of Kāne, named after a healing spring in the area; Ho'onanea, to relax; and Halekula, school house, probably referring to Punahou. These streets have a different story to tell, one I haven't yet learned.

I think this cluster of haole names has a lot to do with the swirls of schools located on Dole Street. Haoles brought the grade- and classroom-centered education model to Hawai'i.

In this sense, Dole is the spine of the reddish centipede. I have even seen several on Dole Street. Centipedes are carnivorous with chewing mouthparts and legs modified into poison claws. They can get over six inches long in Hawaiʻi. When they bite, they leave a permanent black mark.

Starting from my apartment, the first street on the centipede is Frank Street. It goes up the hill from Dole to St. Louis Heights. It is named after Brother Frank who came to Hawaiʻi to teach at St. Louis in 1883.

Then come the series of roads that traverse the university. They are East-West Road, named after the East-West Center; Donaghho Road, named after a math professor at the university during the early part of the century; Bachman Place, named after a president of the university in the 1950s; and University Avenue. Around the university, Dole Street is not so much like a centipede. The geography here is built on a whole series of haole and/or institutional names stacked on top of one another. There are no university buildings named after Hawaiians. Yet up until the student protests a few years ago, the university did see it fit to name a building after Stanley D. Porteus, an Australian who liked to write papers on genetics in which he supposedly proved with maze tests things such as: "the worst defects of Hawaiian temperament are his deficiency of planning capacity, extreme suggestibility, and instability of interest."

Dole Street around the university is a closed system of sorts, one that illustrates how power clusters in close patterns on top of geography, as in the topography map of a volcano crater where the lines are drawn closer and closer together to represent depth, or like those images of the various human circulatory systems in the body that are brightly colored and show interconnected yet separate systems of movement through the body.

At the edge of the university, is Dole Street's one bar, Players. Players waitresses are required to wear short skirts but are not required to have any waitressing experience to get hired. Across the street from Players is Founder's Gate. Founder's Gate is two stone arches with benches on opposite sides of the street. One side of it reads "maluna aʻe o na lahui apau ke ola ke kanaka" and the other reads "above all nations is humanity." I have never seen anyone sit on the benches. But there is no reason to ever sit at this intersection as it is very busy with cars and the benches look very uncomfortable. I like it that the funds for Founder's Gate were raised by 2,664 individuals each donating $1.

After the university, on this side of Dole Street, the sidewalk disappears. Dole Street gets narrower and it is no longer a major thoroughfare. I rarely walk this part of Dole Street. My knowledge of it is more academic than lived.

After the university area comes Wilder Street. Samuel G. Wilder arrived in 1858. Wilder Street used to be called Stonewall. Queen Kaʻahumanu had prisoners build a wall along it in the 1830s. Clerks in Wilder's office petitioned for the change. There isn't much evidence of the wall anymore. Instead this intersection has a lot of fast moving traffic turning onto the H1 freeway. Wilder had a shipping business. He also laid a lot of railroad track for the transportation of sugar cane. He named one of his locomotives Thing of Fire, a name that was given to him when he first arrived. Like most annexationists and haole settlers at the time, he was involved in sugar. Because fate is what it is, or because fate urges us not to celebrate being called a thing of fire, his son fell into a vat of boiling syrup at the sugar mill and died from severe burns.

Then Griffiths Street. Arthur Floyd Griffiths was the principal of

Punahou School at the turn of the century. He was an unremarkable principal. Griffiths is half a block long. It leads into a concrete bunker and a fence. Hibiscus tries to grow along the fence. The fence has signs that say "Guard Dog on Duty" and "Posted: No Trespassing" every two feet. Behind the fence is a lush garden with lots of papaya.

Then Farrington Street. Wallace R. Farrington has a street, a high school, and a highway in his honor. He was the governor of Hawaiʻi from 1921–1929. He established Hawaiʻi's Bill of Rights and Declaration of Rights. The two gave Hawaiʻi federal lands for public education and ended discrimination against Chinese and Japanese citizens who had been unable to travel freely between Hawaiʻi and the continent. Because he was editor of the Evening Bulletin, now the Honolulu Star-Bulletin, there have been several positive historical profiles on him in the paper in the last couple of years. He did fight racism against Japanese and Chinese and the geographical prominence of his name is probably indicative of the emerging alliance between haole and Asian settlers that so defines power in the state today. But he strongly supported annexation. And in 1924 he called the National Guard in on striking Filipino plantation workers. Breaking this strike ended organized resistance against the Big 5 plantations for over a decade.

Then Metcalf Street. Metcalf is named after Theophilus Metcalf. He was involved in a lot of things really early on. He was marshal of the old fort and he also did surveying and financing and sugar milling in the 1830s. His daughter, Emma M. Nakuina, later wrote down the story of the creation of Punahou Spring. This is a big intersection with lots of traffic coming from Waikīkī. Pedestrians are supposed to keep off and use the stairs when they get to Metcalf.

—

43

Then Oliver Street. Oliver P. Emerson does not seem to have done all that much as far as I can figure out, and Oliver Street thus is a small street about four feet away from Metcalf. Emerson was a missionary. But he spent the prime of his life converting those on the continent. He was, however, related to the Emerson family: a family of missionaries and translators. There are two other streets in Honolulu named after the more prominent Emersons: ʻEmekona Street and Emerson Street. Oliver P. Emerson also owned a collection of achatinellidae.

Then Spreckels Street. Claus Spreckels is a much more important person with a much longer street. Spreckels was a California sugar industrialist. His dealings in Hawaiʻi are like the kiawe, and several grow on Spreckels, that was brought to Hawaiʻi in the 1800s as horse feed; with its deep root systems it has lowered the water tables throughout all of Hawaiʻi. Before the overthrow and in an attempt to avoid dealing with the haole settler elites, Kalākaua struck a deal with Spreckels, granting him water rights for sugar in exchange for a cash gift and a loan. This was an attempt by Kalākaua to obtain financing independent from the current system of taxes on haole settlers. His merriness, his spending of his tax money to preserve and extend Hawaiian culture in various ways, was upsetting them. Spreckels was much hated by figures like Dole because he supported Kalākaua over them. Dole parodies Spreckels as Herr Von Boss in his satires. Spreckels was an astute businessman and because of his water rights was able to monopolize the sugar industry in Hawaiʻi for some time. It is said by some that you are "wai wai" if you are a rich man. Or you are, like Spreckels, "water water."

The story of Dole, Spreckels, and Wilder, despite their disagreements, is the story of Hawaiʻi being allowed to modernize only into a one industry town. Kalākaua had a choice between sugar or sugar. Then it was sugar, now it is tourism. Eventually Kalākaua tires of Spreckels's hubris. Kalākaua pays off his loan and then ousts Spreckels. Yet history continues.

Dole Street dead ends into Punahou.

—
45

five

In the story of Punahou, there are twin rain spirits: Kauawaʻahila and Kauakiʻowao. The twins are abused by an evil stepmother and they flee when their father is away. Their stepmother pursues them and as she chases them they run down into the valley and hide right behind where Punahou School is now. They hide for a long time. Eventually, Kauakiʻowao starts to long for a bath.

Kauawaʻahila calls on the moʻo Kakea, a maternal ancestor, who controls the water. A moʻo is a lizard. Kakea is a generous moʻo and not only provides the water for a bath but also diverts some of his water supply to establish a spring there. Kauawaʻahila plants kalo around the spring and this attracts people and it turns into a settlement. This settlement though eventually attracts foreigners who do not respect the water, who plant water lilies from afar in it, who build a church overlooking it. After this, the twins return to the upper reaches of the mountain. In the meantime their father has returned and killed their stepmother and then himself in anger and despair. They rarely return to Punahou. Dennis Kawaharada who tells a different version of this story in Traditions of Oʻahu notices the use value of this story in that it "describes rainfall patterns in Makiki and Mānoa and an innovation in agriculture (digging an irrigation tunnel to make relatively dry lands productive); it also establishes water rights at the new spring."

Dole Street runs along the mouth of the Mānoa valley. The back of the valley is lush because of the rain from Kauawaʻahila and Kauakiʻowao. But Dole Street and its foreigners tends to be drier.

Punahou school has a famous stone fence covered with night blooming cereus, a cactus. A seaman brought the cactus from Acapulco and gave it to a missionary teacher at Punahou years ago. It not only still grows there, but the cereus grows all over the dry areas of Oʻahu. Like many of the plants brought from afar it has taken over. It has a huge white bloom that opens at night and then wilts in the morning sun. Bees are attracted to it.

six

The apartment I rent has cereus growing on a ledge out the bedroom window. It grows up a concrete fence and over the top. The neighbor always knocks it over when it reaches the top. He so does not want anything growing near him that he has paved his whole front yard.

The Mānoa valley is mauka to my house. Kaimukī is makai. Kaimukī is hot and dry. It is a small shield volcano. The word means oven for cooking ki. I do not know what neighborhood I live in really. When people ask I tell them I live at the intersection of Mānoa, Kaimukī, and St. Louis. I live at the intersection of moistness and dryness.

I am obsessed with the cereus out my bedroom window and I watch its buds to make sure I see each one bloom during its season. In the morning after it blooms I go outside and watch the bees that have gathered inside the wilting blooms.

While the story of Dole and Wilder and Spreckels is not my story, I am a part of Dole Street's swirl of connection whether I like it or not. A swirl that is like the system of the separate lines on the topographic map that are inside each other but are not a spiral and never really meet. Like the systems that circulate fluids and energy throughout the body but never mix. I live on Dole Street because I teach at the university.

Punahou school tells the story of its name in its publicity materials but it does not tell Nakuina's version. They tell of an elderly Hawaiian couple who pray for water and are told where to find it in a dream. There is no moʻo who shares his water. There is no settlement as a result. And then no complaint about the foreigners who arrive and build twenty-story hotels.

Dole Street does not lead to any water. Rain avoids it. Near Frank Street is a cistern, but I have never noticed it to be full.

When I walk home from work, at the first vista I see Diamond Head. But by the second vista, the one that will dominate the walk, I can only see the buildings of Waikīkī. The buildings of Waikīkī fascinate me. They are smooth clean buildings, built after the late

47

1960s. They have no fire escapes; no water towers; none of the messiness that defines most cityscapes. While the buildings are of different heights, they all look related. The skyline of Waikīkī is the image of a silent scream.

48
—

seven

It is often said that Hawai'i is unique because of its syncretism. The beautiful colors of the bougainvillea on the hillside above Dole Street are pointed out. The sweet song of the java finch will be mentioned. The quaint cadences of pidgin will be remarked upon. The word "local" will be embraced. The beauty of young girls of indeterminate race or ethnicity will be celebrated. The sweet sounds of songs played on a ukulele will be hummed.

And they will be right that all these things are wonderful.

But what I have learned from walking up and down Dole Street is that one cannot just celebrate syncretism. It comes with a complicated history. For syncretism to matter as a way out of all the separatisms that define us and their potential turns to absolutes, it can't be simple. Simple syncretism has been used again and again in Hawai'i to erase the power dynamics that make it a colonial state. The fact that certain people had to meet the values, languages, and desires of certain others who suddenly arrived because they could not survive otherwise while those who arrived had a choice about whether they would meet the values, languages, and desires of those who were present often gets overlooked.

One could point to how Dole Street runs almost parallel to
Waiʻalae, mudhen water, and Ala Moana, ocean street, and say
how wonderful it is that there is room for the indigenous and the
immigrant in Hawaiʻi's street names. But on Dole Street, names
do not mix. And geographies do not mix as Dole Street marks
the edges of the valley. It is not that Dole Street is an absolute or
successful example of separation. Things meet on Dole Street as
they meet everywhere. It is that Dole Street mainly tells a certain
history, a history of how the arrival of western education and its
separations and refusals to mix came with and was propped up
by settlers who came mainly from the continent and their powers.
It tells a story of unchance meetings. It tells a story of how the
educational system socializes and westernizes more than it adapts
or mixes. And it tells how when those who enter that educational
system change, this change is celebrated as a meeting. It tells an
old story, which is also a current story.

I need to think about Dole Street's history because I am a part
of Dole Street as I walk up and down it. I came to it as part of this
history. As the stereotypical continental schoolteacher, I need to
think about how to respect the water that is there, how not to suck it
all up with my root system, how to make a syncretism that matters,
how to allow fresh water to flow through it, how to acknowledge and
how to change in various unpredictable ways.

The artist Kim Jones walked across Wilshire Boulevard in
Los Angeles one day with a huge apparatus on his back. In the
photographs of the event it is hard to tell exactly what he used
to construct the apparatus but it looks like sticks and mud tied
together in a loose, boxy sort of nest. It looks like the land. The
apparatus appears heavy and unwieldy on him. It extends above his

head and off his back by several feet. He wears some sort of mask that makes his face featureless as he walks. He is generic as he carries his apparatus. In some photographs, Jones draws a version of this apparatus over images of himself. One shows him crouching in Dong Ha Vietnam in full camouflage with the apparatus drawn on his head.

Kim Jones, in carrying a heavy and unwieldy nest, on his back out in public, might have an answer.

Nests draw things together and have many points of contact. They swirl into a new thing. All sorts of items end up in them. I found one the other day on Dole Street that was full of twigs and leaves and feathers and gum and plastic string.

Sources

Daws, Gavin. *Shoal of Time: A History of the Hawaiian Islands.* Honolulu: U of
Hawaii P, 1974.

Hargreaves, Dorothy and Bob. *Hawaii Blossoms.* Lahaina: Ross-Hargreaves,
1958.

Jones, Kim. "Wilshire Boulevard Walk." *Chain 8* (2000). 98-99.

Kawaharada, Dennis. *Traditions of O'ahu: Stories of an Ancient Land.* leahi.kcc.
hawaii.edu/~dennisk/Oahu/welcome.html.

Kobayashi, Victor N., ed. *Building a Rainbow: A History of the Buildings and
Grounds of the University of Hawaii-Mānoa Campus.* Mānoa: U of Hawai'i, Mānoa/
Hui O Students, 1983.

Pukui, Mary, Samuel Elbert, and Esther T. Mookini. *Place Names of Hawaii.*
Honolulu: U of Hawaii P, 1974.

Smith, Clifford. *Hawaiian Alien Plant Studies.* www.botany.hawaii.edu/faculty/
cw_smith/aliens.htm.

Vann, Michael G. "Contesting Cultures and Defying Dependency: Migration,
Nationalism, and Identity in Late 19th Century Hawaii." *The Stanford Humanities
Review* 5.2 (1997): 146-173.

Watten, Barrett. *Bad History.* Berkeley: Atelos, 1998.

—

51

PHOTOGRAPHS BY JULIANA SPAHR

N **21°** 18' 28" W **157°** 48' 28"

Things of Each Possible Relation Hashing Against One Another

N **40°** 41' 5" W **73°** 58' 8"

the view from the sea

the constant motion of claiming, collecting, changing, and taking

the calmness of bays and the greenness of land caused by the
    freshness of things growing into

the arrival to someplace else

the arrival to someplace differently

the freshness of the things increasing

the greenness of the ground

the calmness of the compartments

the constant movement to claim, to gather, to change, and to
    consider sea

the arrival to someplace differently

constant motion

the green of the soil which increases the freshness of things

then calmness and the sail

the requirement on meeting to modify and to regard

the inbound of this someplace differently

the constant movement

the green of the ground that magnifies the coolness of the things

the calmness and the sail

the cause, the modifies, and the sea stops considering

the requirement in the meeting

the entrance with this someplace differently

things in constant movement

and from the green of the earth which it magnifies for coolness

considering from calmness and from ventilation

and the sea is modified

the requirements of this meeting
that this is someplace differently
the input of information
the coolness of things in constant movement
and the green of the track
from this calmness is the breath and the ventilation
the sea is modified and urges considerations
and then the conditions in the cause of meeting
the input of information that this is someplace differently
then the coolness and the things in constant motion
to this calmness there is the breath and the green of the land
the sea expands and is modified by considerations

what we know is like and unalike
as it is kept in different shaped containers
it is as the problems of analogy
it as the view from the sea
it is as the introduction of plants and animals, others, exotically
yet it is also as the way of the wood borer
and the opinion of the sea
as it is as the occidental concepts of government, commerce,
    money and imposing
what we know is like and unalike
one stays diverse with formed packages
that is what the problems of the analogy are

the problems of the sight from the sea

and the problems of the introduction of koa haole and axis
    deer

yet also like the way of the snipe

the sight of the sea

the great and extremely fast modifications of a series

is what we know, is like and unalike

whereas one remains forming diverse assemblies

whereas the problems of the analogy are still

as the sight of the sea

as the introduction of factories and animals, foreign, exotic

yet also like the way of the plover

also like the vision from the sea

as well as western concepts of government, trade, money, and
    imposition

what we know is like and unalike

whereas one continues being diverse formed assemblies

whereas the problems of the analogy

whereas the sight of the sea

whereas the introduction of tree of heaven and cow

also continue being like the way of the a`o

then again the sight of the sea

again a series of great and extremely fast changes

what us knows is like and unalike

as we continues to be the various formed assemblies

as the sight of the sea

as the introduction of exotic, alien plants and animals

becomes the sea of the way
the sight of the sight
and the introduction of mongoose and apple snail
is the sight of the sight of the sea of the stroke

analogy from analogy
analogy of analogy
caterpillar of the moth
ant of the dragonfly
grub of the grasshopper
connection from connection
pinworm of the fly
connection of the connection
egg of the bird
link of the link
life from life
connection of connection
life from the life
life of the lifespan
it can't be otherwise
life of the life span
it cannot be of another way
it cannot be of another way
duration of the duration of the life
it cannot be from another way

snipe of the plover
it cannot be in another manner
a`o of the a`u
turnstone of the flycatcher
it cannot be in an other way
mudhen of the apapane
earthworm from grub
crow from alawi
worm of the food
worm of food
`e`ea from alaaiha
continuous screw of the food

then the opening of the things sewn together
the opening of shifting the analogy of the opening
also the paginations of the commands of the things
like the cells in the wings of the branch and the cells in the veins
    of the paginations of the units impelling
you estimate sonar of the dolphin and sonar of the branch
like the part of the extremity of the bird and the part of the
    extremity of the dolphin
like the wing of the butterfly and the bird
like hummingbird the aspiration and the aspiration of the
    butterfly
like the language humans of nature and hummingbird the
    language

as newt the wing under the amphibians and lizard under the
        reptiles
as the taste of the eyes lizard and the eyes of humans
making the analogy slide to the opening of the paginations of the
        commandos of the things
around the night to connect doubled from the branch
like the language of the human being and the hummingbird of
        the language
like the hummingbird of the aspiration and the aspiration of the
        butterfly
like the wings of the butterfly and the bird
like the part of the extremity of the bird and the part of the
        extremity of the dolphin
appreciate sonar of the dolphin and sonar of the jump
like the cells in the wings of the jump and the cells in the veins of
        the paginations of the mechanisms impelling
and the cells in the veins of the pilot of the paginations
to join the night doubled of the ramification
sliding the analogy of the opening of the paginations of the
        controls of the things
as newt the wing under the amphibians and the lizard under the
        reptiles has taste of the eyes of the lizard and the eyes of
        the human
whereas the cells in the veins of the pilot of the paginations
like the cells in the wings of the blowing and the cells in the veins
        of the paginations of impelling mechanisms
like the sonar of the dolphin and the sonar of the blowing

like the piece of the end of the bird and the piece of the end of
    the dolphin
like the wings of the butterfly and the bird
like hummingbird of the suction and the suction of the butterfly
like the language of the human being and hummingbird of the
    language
as newt the wing under the amphibians and the lizard under
    reptiles has taste of the eyes of the lizard and the eyes of
    the human being
slipping the analogy of the opening of things
join the night of doubled ramification
like eyes of the lizard and eyes of the human
like language of human and hummingbird the language
as a hummingbird of suction and suction of butterfly
like wings of the butterfly and the bird
like piece of the end of the bird and piece of the end of the
    dolphin
like sonar of the dolphin and sonar of the blow
like cells in the wings of the blow and cells in the veins of the
    pages
whereas the cells in the veins of the pages pilot and
controls pages together the night of branch bent
sliding the analogy of the opening of the things
while the cells in the veins of pages drive and
like newt the wing under the amphibians and the lizard under
    reptiles

as the cells in the wings of the blow and the cells in the veins of
     drives pages
as the sonar of the dolphin and the sonar of the blow
as the end piece of the bird and the end piece of the dolphin
as the wings of the butterfly and of the bird
as sucking hummingbird and sucking butterfly
as the tongue of humans and the tongue of hummingbird
as the eyes of the lizard and the eyes of humans
as newt the wing under amphibians and the lizard under reptiles
night gliding from analogy
drives pages together on the branch, night sewn
as the newt among amphibians and the lizard among reptiles
as the eyes of the lizard and the eyes of the human
as the tongue of the human and the tongue of the hummingbird
as the sucking of the hummingbird and the sucking of the
     butterfly
as the wings of the butterfly and the wings of the bird
as the tail of the bird and the tail of the dolphin
as the sonar of the dolphin and the sonar of the bat
as the cells in the wings of the bat and the cells in the veins of the
     leaves
as the cells in the veins of the leaves and the leaves on the
     branches
the opening of the things sewn together

so it was and so it is

endless screw of the feeding

it was so and so it is

it was thus and thus it is

screw without aim of the feeding

it was therefore and therefore is it

so we will be

it was consequently and consequently is it

we will be so

we will be thus

it was consequently and consequently it is

therefore we are

we are consequently

we are consequently

so we are

alaaiha, `e`ea, alawi, crow, apapane, mudhen

we are so

bird, egg, fly, pinworm, grasshopper, grub

we are thus

fly-catcher, turnstone, a`u, a`o, plover, snipe

therefore we are

dragonfly, ant, moth, caterpillar, woodborer

we are consequently

we are consequently

while the problems of the analogy

also continue to be as the way of the a`u

and the series of large and extremely rapid changes

turns into the view of the view

brings the introduction of the factories and the animals, other,
    exotically

and the sight of the track

even as one continues to be the various formed assemblies which
    are

the problems of the analogy

and even as one also continues to be the seeing of the turnstone

western concepts of government, trade, cash and imposing

the vision from the track

then the introduction of ant and coconut heart rot

while what we are knows the unalike and

while one becomes the various compositions formed by nature

the problems of the analogy

are the sight of the trace

and nature as the way to see the fly-catcher

and the series of large and extremely fast modifications

in the sight of the land

and the introduction of the plants and the animals, others, exotic

when it is we, it is the unalike knowing and

if one were to transform nature's given forms

then the problems of the analogy of it appear

while the way to see it is as mudhen

the sight from the earth

the concepts western of the government, commerce, money and
    great modifications
and then the opinion from the country
and then the introduction of the greenhouse frog and the myna
and then again the sight of the track
and then the extremely fast shutdowns of a series
and then the view from the land
if it is we, if it is unalike the known and
if one forms nature to convert something into structure
then the problems of the analogy of nature also convert
we ask how to see the line of the crow

so there is
the view from land
the firm steadiness of earth
all its plants and all its fresh waters together
the hull of a boat
and then there is its bough and its sail and its movement toward
its movement toward things from somewhere else
the ground
the lack of firm regularity of the ground
all its factories and all its fresh waters
the hull of a boat and its bough and its sail and its movement toward
things some share differently
the lack of fixed uniformity of soil

all this, factories and fresh waters

the trunk of a boat and its bough and its sail and its movement
toward

things of different proportion

the lack of fixed uniformity of the ground

all its plants and everything and its units of cool waters

the trunk of a boat and its bough and its sail and its movement

things of any ratio differently than the one

the mountain range

the lack of uniformity fixes the earth

all their plants and all the fresh water

the trunk of a boat and its bough and its candle and its never
shutdown movement

things of any relation differently transformed

the interval of mountain

the difficulties of uniformity

the ground and all the factories and all the units of fresh water

the network of a boat and of sound bough and the candle and the
never stop of the movement

things of any relation transformed to be different than that one

the distance of the mountain

the difficulties of the regularity of the soil and all their factories
and all the units of fresh water

a boat and the sound bough and the candle and the impact of
movement

things of each possible relation and the transformation

in the distance the mountain

difficulties of regularity suppressed

the ground and all this, its plants and everything, its units of cool

    waters

a boat and bough healthy and its candle and its impact of

    movement

things of each possible relation differently

in the distance of the mountain

the suppressed difficulties of the earth

regularity and all this

plants and all their fresh water

a boat, a bough and a candle

impact movement

things of each possible relation hashing against one another

—

67

Shortly after I moved to Hawai'i I began to loudly and hubristically
proclaim whenever I could that nature poetry was immoral. There
is a lot of nature poetry about Hawai'i. Much of it is written by those
who vacation here and it is often full of errors. Rob Wilson calls these
poems 747 poems. These poems often show up in the New Yorker or
various other establishment journals. But I was more suspicious of
nature poetry because even when it got the birds and the plants and
the animals right it tended to show the beautiful bird but not so often
the bulldozer off to the side that was destroying the bird's habitat. And
it wasn't talking about how the bird, often a bird which had arrived
recently from somewhere else, interacted with and changed the larger
system of this small part of the world we live in and on.

By the time Captain Cook was traveling the Pacific, botanical artists
were a crucial part of colonial exploration. Most ships had at least
one on board. They made drawings of isolated plants against white
backgrounds. The drawings are undeniably beautiful. But there is
little reference to where the plants grow or what grows near them or
what birds rested in them or ate their seeds and fruits or what bees
or moths came to spread their pollen or how humans used them or
avoided them. I saw nature poetry as being in this tradition of isolation.

So during the summer of 2001 I took an ethnobotany course in order to
learn otherwise. I also took an ethnobotany course because
I was trying to be a better poet. I was trying to learn more about
the world and the world around me was so rich with plants
and animals and birds and yet so many of them were dying at such
unprecedented rates. I was trying to think more about nature poetry.

The juxtaposition between the great beauty of Hawai'i and how it is also a huge ecological catastrophe with the highest rates of species extinction and endangerment in the United States was always emotionally confusing to me. I couldn't reconcile the coolness of the breeze and the sweet smells from the flowers and the beauty of cliffs and sea with the large amount of death that was happening. And I was also thinking at the time about how poets need to know the names of things and I didn't really know the names of lots of things that grew in Hawai'i. I also didn't know where they came from. I knew that when I looked around anywhere on the islands that most of what I was seeing had come from somewhere else but I didn't know where or when. I was not yet seeing how the deeper history of contact was shaping the things I saw around me. That summer I read Isabella Aiona Abbott's La'au Hawai'i: Traditional Hawaiian Uses Of Plants, *E.S. Craighill Handy and Elizabeth Green Handy's* Native Planters in Old Hawaii, *and Martha Warren Beckwith's translation of the* Kumulipo, *Dennis Kawaharada's* Storied Landscapes: Hawaiian Literature and Place, *Daniel Nettle and Suzanne Romaine's* Vanishing Voices: The Extinction of the World's Languages, *Greg Dening's* Islands and Beaches: Discourse on a Silent Land: Marquesas, 1774–1880. *And also a number of resources on the web such as* 'Āinakumuwai: Ahupua'a of Nāwiliwili Bay *(www.hawaii.edu/environment/ ainakumuwai/index.htm),* Na Meakanu o Wa'a o Hawai'i Kahiko *(www. canoeplants.com), and Gerald Carr's listing of plants in Hawai'i (www. botany.hawaii.edu/faculty/carr/default.htm). All this writing by others is in these poems.*

*I wrote first drafts of many of these poems during class lectures
in Ethnobotany 101. After I wrote first drafts, I put the drafts through
the altavista translation machine (world.altavista.com) and translated
my English words between the languages that came to the Pacific
from somewhere else: French, Spanish, German, and Portuguese. The
translation machine is of course full of flaws and offers back some
sort of language that only alludes to sense because it is so connected
with another language. I like this about it. Then, after I had a number
of different versions of the same poem, I sat down and wove them
together. I wanted to weave them into complicated, unrecognizable
patterns. I took the patterns from the math that shows up in plants. Or
I tried to approximate the shapes of things I saw around me.*

*Greg Dening argues that there are two views that define the
Pacific: a view from the sea (the view of those who arrived from
elsewhere) and the view from the land (those who were already there).
These poems open with the view from the sea and end with the view
from the land and are about the hashing that happens as these two
views meet. Mixed in with these two views is this quote from Abbott:
"The introduction of exotic (alien) plants and animals as well as
Western concepts of government, trade, money, and taxation began a
series of large and extremely rapid changes."*

*Around the time I was working on this, Jonathan Skinner started
publishing his journal* Ecopoetics. *And then I realized that what I was
looking for all along was in the tradition of ecopoetics—a poetics full
of systemic analysis that questions the divisions between nature and
culture—instead of a nature poetry.*

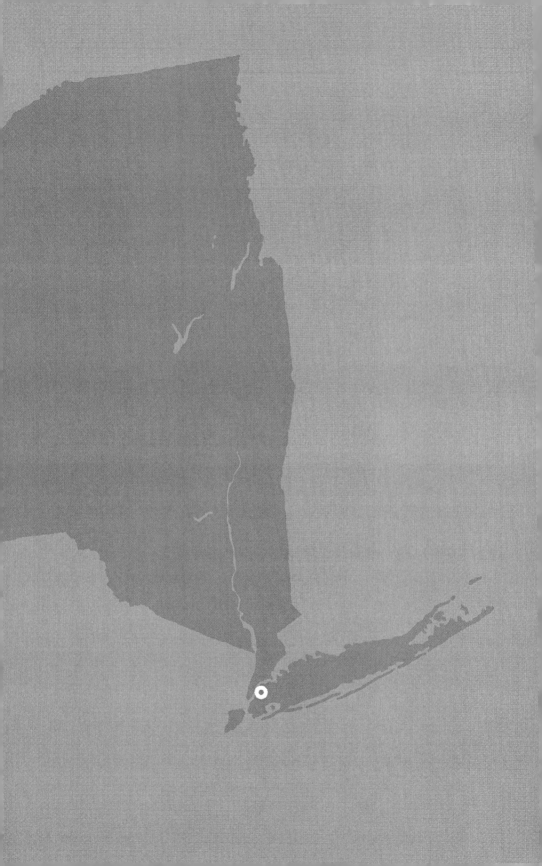

N **40°** 41' 5" W **73°** 58' 8"

Unnamed Dragonfly Species

The city of Rotterdam sent over daffodils. **A Noctuid Moth** The
daffodils bloomed in the first weeks of April. **Allegheny Woodrat**
They were everywhere. **American Bittern** They were yellow.
American Burying Beetle It was April and then the temperature
was 90 degrees and all the daffodils died immediately. **Arogos
Skipper** All at the same time. **Atlantic Hawksbill Sea Turtle** This
happened right where they were living. **Atlantic Ridley Sea Turtle** It
was early April. **Bald Eagle**

In November of the previous year a big piece of the Antarctic Pine Island glacier broke off. **Banded Sunfish** A crack had formed in the glacier in the middle of the previous year. **Barrens Buckmoth** And then by November the piece had just broken off. **Bicknell's Thrush** It had just taken a few months from crack to breaking point. **Black Rail** The iceberg that was formed was twenty-six miles by ten miles. **Black Redhorse** Then in the following March, the March of the same year of the 90 degree early April, the Larsen B ice shelf shattered and separated from the Antarctic Peninsula. **Black Skimmer** All of this happened far away from them. **Black Tern** They had never even been near Antarctica. **Blanding's Turtle**

They heard about all this cracking and breaking away on the news and then they began to search over the internet for information on what was going on. **Blue Whale** On the internet they found an animation of the piece of the Antarctic Pine Island glacier breaking off. **Bluebreast Darter** After they found this, they often called this animation up and just watched it over and over on their screen in their dimly lit room. **Blue-spotted Salamander** In the animation, which was really just a series of six or so satellite photographs, a crack would appear in the middle of the glacier. **Bog Buckmoth** Then a few frames later the crack would widen and extend itself toward the edges and then the piece would break off. **Bog Turtle** They wondered often about the details. **Brook Floater Buffalo Pebble Snail** What does this breaking off sound like? **Canada Lynx** Or what it was like to be there on the piece that was breaking off. **Cerulean Warbler** Did waves form? **Checkered White** Was there a tsunami? **Chittenango Ovate Amber Snail** What had it been like for the penguins or the fish? **Clubshell**

On the internet they realized that Iceland's Vatnajokull glacier is melting by about three feet a year. **Common Loon** That the Bering Glacier in Alaska recently lost as much as seven and a half miles in a sixty day period. **Common Nighthawk** That the European Alps lost half their ice over the last century and that many of the rivers of Europe were likely to be gone in twenty to thirty years time. **Common Sanddragon** That the Columbia Glacier in Alaska will continue to recede, possibly at a rate of as much as ten miles in ten years. **Common Tern** That thirty-six cubic miles of ice had melted from glaciers in West Antarctica in the past decade and that alone had raised sea levels worldwide by about one-sixtieth of an inch. **Cooper's Hawk** That on Mt. Rainier warmer temperatures were causing the ice to melt under the glacier and this caused water to suddenly burst out of the glacier and race down the mountain. **Cougar** That tropical ice caps were disappearing even faster. **Deepwater Sculpin** That a glacier on the Quelccaya ice cap is retreating by five hundred feet per year. **Dwarf Wedgemussel** That Kilimanjaro in East Africa has lost eighty-two percent of its area in eighty-eight years. **Eastern Box Turtle** That Pakistan was thinking about melting their glacier so they could get some more water for their people although this was not recommended by the United

Nations and might not actually happen. **Eastern Hognose Snake**
They learned that all this melting began to accelerate in 1988.
Eastern Sand Darter That the rate of ice lost had doubled
since 1988. **Eastern Spadefoot Toad** That 1988 was a sort of turning
point year as it was the beginning of each year being the hottest
year on record year after year. **Eastern Spiny Softshell**

They had been alive in 1988. **Eskimo Curlew** They could not even
remember thinking at all about the weather that year. **Extra
Striped Snaketail** When they really thought about it, they had no
memory of any year being any hotter than any other year in general.
Fat Pocketbook They remembered a few hot summers and a
few mild winters but they were more likely to remember certain
specific storms like the blizzard of 1976. **Fence Lizard** They did not
remember heat as glaciers remember heat, deep in the center,
causing cracking or erupting. **Finback Whale** They had spent 1988
living in various parts of the country. **Fringed Valvata** None of them
knew each other in 1988. **Frosted Elfin** Some of them were involved
with other people. **Gilt Darter** Some of them thought about finishing
college and getting jobs. **Golden Eagle** Yet some just thought about
hitting baseballs. **Golden-winged Warbler** At various moments
they joined each other and many others in thinking about Pan Am
flight 103 that had exploded over Lockerbie, Scotland. **Grasshopper
Sparrow** And then again they all noticed on the same day when the
U.S. shot down Iran Air Flight 655, supposedly by accident, in the
Persian Gulf. **Gravel Chub** And several of them did not go to the
beach in 1988 because the beach near them was in New Jersey and
that year beaches in New Jersey were closed because of medical

waste coming ashore. **Gray Petaltail** Some of them were trying to rid themselves of drunk boyfriends and thought so much about this that there was little room for thinking about other things like the warmth or beaches. **Gray Wolf** And some of them were living for part of that year right at the edge of where the Wisconsin glacier had ended thousands of years ago and the town in which they lived had a flat part and a hilly part as a result but even though the geography of their daily life was so clearly formed by a glacier they didn't really think about the warm year and things melting. **Green Floater** Some of them worked at an anarchist bookstore. **Green Sea Turtle** Some of them had tans that summer that they got from walking around outside because they needed to be outside walking around in order to think about how best to be somewhat content in this life right now. **Grizzled Skipper** Some of them drove cabs. **Harbor Porpoise** None of them really fell in love but some of them had lovers. **Hart's-Tongue Fern**

After the piece of the Antarctic Pine Island glacier broke off, they could not stop thinking about glaciers and the way they thought about glaciers the most was by reading about them on the internet late at night, their eyes blurring and their shoulders tight. **Hellbender** There they sometimes found arguments from the side that the oil drillers celebrated, the side that said the melting did not matter. **Henry's Elfin** Sometimes, if it was really late at night and if they had written on a small notepad beside their computer an especially long list of things that were melting as they tended to do, they would read this argument liked by oil drillers and try to be reassured by the information that if the Antarctic Pine Island glacier melted away it didn't matter much because it would only raise sea levels by a quarter of an inch. **Henslow's Sparrow** A quarter of an inch they would think. **Herodias Underwing** A quarter of an inch does not matter. **Hessel's Hairstreak** Then questions would surface through this blurry comfort of small amounts of rising ocean. **Horned Lark** Would the Antarctic Pine Island glacier melt just on its own, they would wonder? **Houghton's Goldenrod** Wouldn't the Vatnajokull also be melting at the same time? **Humpback Whale** And the alps and the tropical ice caps and the poles? **Indiana Bat** And then they read that while a quarter of an inch does not seem like much, a rise of one foot of ocean level typically means that shorelines end up one hundred feet or more inland. **Ironcolor Shiner** A sea rise of just three feet in Bangladesh would put one half of that nation underwater, displacing more than one hundred million people. **Jair Underwing** Already on the nine islands of Tuvalu farmers must grow their plants in containers because the rising sea level has seeped into the ground water. **Jefferson Salamander** The four nations of Tuvalu, Kiribati, Marshall Islands, and Tokelau Islands, each made up of many islands, will most certainly be entirely displaced in the next thirty years. **Karner Blue**

They themselves tended to live on islands and thinking about what this meant had provoked them to think so much about this rising ocean level and then to feel that the breaking off of the Antarctic Pine Island glacier was all about them, or not all about them but as having a scary relevance to their lives. **King Rail** They often lived on an island in the Pacific and they often lived on an island in the Atlantic. **Lake Chubsucker** They thought of these two residences of theirs as opposites although both were places of great economic privilege and resources, places that themselves consumed large amounts of resources and consumed more and more resources all the time. **Lake Sturgeon** One preferred to think of itself as local and often as in resistance to the United States and one preferred to think of itself as international and often as the center of finance and culture for the United States. **Least Bittern** One had a smallish city and one had one of the largest cities in the world. **Least Tern** One was six hundred square miles and one was twenty-six square miles. **Leatherback Sea Turtle** Both were likely to feel the effects of the rising ocean although many of the residents of both were pretending that what was happening to the nations of Tuvalu, Kiribati, Marshall Islands, and Tokelau Islands did not really foretell anything relevant to them at all. **Leedy's Roseroot** Often late at night to allay their worries, they tried to see climate change as just one more tendency of life towards change. **Little Bluet** They tried to look forward to the new fjord that would be created by the receding Columbia glacier in Alaska. **Loggerhead Sea Turtle** They were fascinated by fjords and there will soon be a new one to visit in ten years they would say to themselves. **Loggerhead Shrike** Perhaps even new plants would evolve there. **Longear Sunfish** Or they tried to be comforted about how they grew up in a town that was located right at the edge of where the Wisconsin glacier had ended its journey. **Longhead Darter** And because it had ended there the soil in this area was especially rich as the glacier pushed topsoil before it as it moved, then dumped it right where the town was now. **Longtail Salamander** For years they had eaten off the wealth of the glacier as their family had lived in the hilly section of town and had grown a vegetable garden in the backyard in the rich topsoil. **Marbled Salamander** Or they liked to think about the scientist who claimed that in terms of patterns of heating and cooling on the earth's surface, the earth should be entering a new ice age. **Massasauga** It is long overdue he claimed. **Mooneye** Yet, according to him, this ice age has been perhaps counteracted by human climatic interference. **Mossy Valvata** So maybe we were better off, maybe better fire than ice although who knew what gods or demons were being angered and what they would do with their anger. **Mottled Duskywing**

They were not scientists and could not figure out what to blame or what the long term consequences might be and even if they were scientists they might not be able to figure this out. **Mountain Brook Lamprey** They made no claim to answers they just noticed things. **Mud Sunfish** And the more they read the more confused they became. **Mud Turtle** And at this moment in their lives there was more to read than ever before and it was easier than ever before to acquire as it came through their computers and all the time the computers had newer and better search engines making more and more specific information easier to find. **New England Cottontail** They knew there were certain enemies in this story, such as Bush with his refusal to sign the Kyoto Accord, and certain industries. **Northeastern Beach Tiger Beetle** But they also knew that the Kyoto Accord was too little too late. **Northern Cricket Frog** They also knew that they didn't want to let excessive information paralyze them. **Northern Goshawk** Or excessive guilt. **Northern Harrier** They felt they had to say that they knew that they were in part responsible for it, whatever it was that was causing this, because they lived in the place that used the largest amount of the stuff most likely to cause this warming. **Northern Wild Monk's-hood** They lived among those who used the most stuff up, who burned the most stuff, who

produced the most stuff, and other things like that. **Olympia Marble**
And even if they tried to live their lives with less stuff than others,
they still benefited and were a part of the system that produced all
this stuff and because of this they had a hard time figuring out how
to move beyond their own personal renewed commitment to denial
of stuff and yet their awareness of how they benefited daily from
being a part of the system that used up the most stuff. **Osprey**

So glaciers were not near them but they obsessed them. **Peregrine Falcon** They wondered if it was because of a story a friend had once told them. **Persius Duskywing** She had gone hiking with her uncle and her sister. **Pied-billed Grebe** They had hiked up to a glacier. **Pine Barrens Bluet** On the way there she got tired and her uncle had picked her up and put her on his shoulder. **Pine Pinion Moth** She was tall when they arrived at the glacier. **Pink Mucket** They arrived at the glacier and she could see it and it had a special light she said. **Piping Plover** It had a special light and this special light and its coldness had been so intense to her. **Pugnose Shiner Pygmy Snaketail** The sun in her eyes. **Queen Snake** The special light. **Rayed Bean** The coldness. **Redfin Shiner** All of it had comforted her. **Red-headed Woodpecker** And when she told this story she had started to cry and they had not understood why she had begun to cry in her telling of a story of comfort. **Red-shouldered Hawk** She had told them her story before they began to stay up late at night encountering glaciers on their computer screen, before they watched over and over the animation of the Antarctic Pine Island glacier breaking off. **Regal Fritillary** Before they began to enter the word "glacier" into Google over and over. **Right Whale** Before they thought about their relationship with things big and cold and full of fresh water. **Roseate Tern** Now they found her story intense and moving and often dwelled on it while looking at the animation of the Antarctic Pine Island glacier breaking off. **Round Whitefish** They envied her for touching a glacier, something that mattered so much in everyone's lives even though so few people had had actual contact with it. **Sandplain Gerardia** She knew this thing that was about their life, about everyone's life, in a way they did not. **Scarlet Bluet**

Sometimes they thought that glaciers interested them because glaciers are like zombies: slow moving and full of stuff, full of stuff and can't be stopped. **Seabeach Amaranth** Like how in movies you can put a bunch of knives and bullets in a zombie and it keeps on moving. **Seaside Sparrow** That is how they thought of glaciers. **Sedge Wren Sei Whale** They move and no one can stop them whichever way they go. **Sharp-shinned Hawk** You can't pin them down and hold them in place. **Short-eared Owl** Nor can you deter them when they start moving. **Shortnose Sturgeon** And they have history. **Silver Chub** They have water in layers sort of like a tree's yearly cycles. **Small-footed Bat** As they melt, things embedded in them are uncovered. **Southern Leopard Frog** In one, a British warplane. **Southern Sprite** In others, various tools or buildings or humans from other times. **Sperm Whale** And glaciers have sixty-six percent of the world's fresh water. **Spoonhead Sculpin** That also interested them as many political struggles of the early part of the previous century involved fresh water and they also figured this was going to be true of the current century as fresh water was getting to be more and more necessary as more and more people lived on the earth and as they lived they polluted more and more of the fresh water and used up more and more of the fresh water stored in various underground water tables and developed more and more sophisticated pumps. **Spotted Darter** Already, but a few years into this new century, there were water riots in various parts of the continent on which they lived. **Spotted Turtle** Water is a force and a resource. **Spruce Grouse** Glaciers are water. **Streamline Chub** And it was April and it was in the 90s. **Swamp Darter** How could they not think about things melting all the time? **Tawny Crescent**

They tried to balance out all their anxiety with loud attempts at celebrations of life. **Tiger Salamander** They tried to do this in often ineffectual ways. **Timber Rattlesnake** They might make out in public while standing in line at the grocery or just drink too much with friends and thus stay out late chatting happily in a dark smoky room where there was no evidence of any glacier or any rising ocean level or even any air really or maybe they would just go home and smoke some pot and lie on their bed watching shows about nature on the television with the sound off and think about how soft the bed can feel at such moments, how deep it could let them enter at such moments, or they might talk loudly and excitedly with friends about the latest blockbuster summer movie as if that really mattered to them and they could live with the changing landscape because they had things like movies and books and friends and drugs, things that were common in cities and when in the cities they liked to tell themselves that this was enough, that these things were good enough so that the melting didn't matter. **Tomah Mayfly** They were anxious and were covering things over. **Unnamed Dragonfly Species** They were anxious and they were paralyzed by the largeness and the connectedness of systems, a largeness of relation that they liked to think about and often

celebrated but now seemed unbearably tragic. **Upland Sandpiper**
The connected relationship between water and land seemed deeply
damaged, perhaps beyond repair in numerous places. **Vesper
Sparrow** The systems of relation between living things of all sorts
seemed to have become in recent centuries so hierarchically
human that things not human were dying at an unprecedented rate.
Wavy-rayed Lampmussel And the systems of human governments
and corporations felt so large and unchangeable and so distant
from them yet the effects of their actions felt so connected and so
immediate to what was happening. **Whip-poor-will** They knew this
but didn't know what else to do. **Wood Turtle** And so they just went
on living while talking loudly. **Worm Snake** Living and watching on a
screen things far away from them melting. **Yellow-breasted Chat**

—

93

N **21°** 15' 57" W **157°** 48' 52"

2199 Kalia Road

one

The center of this essay, but not really its subject, is 2199 Kalia Road
in Waikīkī. That is the address of the Halekulani. The Halekulani
is one of the fancier hotels in Waikīkī. Rooms range from $325 to
$4,500 a night. It is, of course, right on the beach.

The beach is the subject of this essay. Or getting to the beach. To
get to the beach from the Halekulani there are three ways.

One way is through the hotel. The hotel is restricted to guests.
You can walk through it and if you look like a tourist or a shopper
no one is likely to stop you. Access to the hotel is policed by a series
of signs that constantly remind you that if you look a little funny
—a little down on your luck, say, or a little ragged around the edges—
then this isn't the place for you.

Signs that tell you not to do things are very popular in Hawaiʻi.
For a few years I took snapshots of all the signs around the

university that were policing behavior. Sometimes classrooms
at the university have as many as four signs on one wall telling
students and faculty what to do or not—please do not eat or drink;
please kokua and replace the chairs in rows; turn out the lights
when leaving; remember to erase the board; don't smoke. I ended
up with a huge number of photographs of signs.

In Waikīkī the signs are constantly reminding everyone that the
land is owned, that it isn't really public.

Even if you aren't staying at the hotel, legally, all beaches in
Hawai'i are public property. Supposedly, the state owns the beach
up to the high water mark.

However, what this means in terms of access is open to debate.

Some argue that the public have the right to pass over private
land to get to the beach.

Some argue that the state has to purchase beach access routes
from property owners and compensate them.

In 2001, the island of Kauai finally declared that anyone subdividing land adjoining either a beach or a mountain area used for recreation had to build trails through property no less than 300 feet or more than 1,500 feet apart.

I can't find any record of such a law on Oʻahu.

The confusion benefits property owners. And to prevent being on the losing side of a court case that might recognize assumed public right of ways in the future, property owners post a lot of restrictive signs. The goal is to suggest that going through the hotel is not a public right of way.

two

There are public access corridors on either side of the entrance to the Halekulani at the base of Lewers street.

When you follow the public access sign to the left, you walk by the front entrance of the Halekulani. And then past a series of locked doors.

The doors of course remind one yet again that this is private property and that there is no beach access.

Once you are past these doors, the beach access is marked with a sign. It is surrounded by three no parking and tow away signs. The nearest parking to this beach access is several blocks away and is short term meters. The nearest parking for more than an hour or so is about four blocks up Lewers. The Halekulani will let you park in their huge parking lot (the building behind the sign), but it costs something like $6–7 an hour.

—
101

Often hotel receptionists, especially for hotels that are not in Waikīkī and that are selling exclusivity, brag to potential guests that the parking spaces for the general public are a long walk away from the hotel and there aren't that many of them so not that many local people are on their beaches.

three

The public beach access corridor is what we used to call in the
midwest a rape corridor. It is narrow and not lit at night. There are
huge exhaust fans from the Halekulani all down the corridor and
they make so much noise that no one could hear you scream.

At the end of the corridor, right on the beach, is a storage area.

Beyond the concession stand is the public beach. Despite this
being a public beach, a catamaran company has set up a business
that takes up most of the beach.

The beach isn't very appetizing. There isn't really room for
sitting, especially with so many people walking through or getting
on the boat.

The beach soon disappears into the water and the Sheraton has
built up a sea wall with a walkway that they restrict to their
guests (although again, as long as you look like a tourist, no one
stops you from walking here; they just could if they wanted to
do so at some point).

four

The public access corridor to the right of the Halekulani is very similar but a little bit dirtier.

Employees of the Halekulani enter the hotel along this access corridor. They often sit in the corridor and smoke. The Halekulani has posted a series of rules on the door.

Like the corridor to the left, this corridor is filled with loud exhaust fans. A few trees grow along the dirt on the edge of the walkway. Because the bar and hotel beside the Halekulani uses the corridor to remove its garbage and wash its bar mats, bits of fruit rind and other sorts of garbage collect in the dirt.

five

I always make it a point to indulge in the myths of Waikīkī as much as possible. Whenever anyone comes to Waikīkī I take them to the Halekulani for a mai tai because the guidebooks tell me these are the best mai tais in the islands.

I begin by parking on Kuhio and Lewers where I put twenty-five cents for every fifteen minutes in the meter no matter what the time of day or night.

Then I walk down Lewers. Lewers is a uniquely dingy street in Waikīkī that is often called Sewers.

Lewers is named after either Christopher H. Lewers, a lawyer from the late 1800s, or Mr. and Mrs. Robert Lewers, the owners of the Halekulani in the same era. The entrance to the Halekulani is at the end of Lewers.

Lewers is full of bars and tourist shops selling "I got lei'd in

Hawaii" t-shirts, plastic hula dolls with bobble hips, and baseball caps celebrating the end of WWII. It is, like all of Waikīkī, also full of weird corridors and alleys that lead to bars and various sorts of shops that are not directly on the street. These are not listed in the Halekulani's list of places to visit.

None of the Halekulani's publicity mentions that the hotel is surrounded by bars that cater to hard-drinking Australians. There is a whole economy in Waikīkī built around Australians and alcohol and busses. Companies sell pub crawls mainly to Australians and their sales representatives often meet the busses coming in from the airports and ask everyone getting off them if they are Australian or not. If they get a yes, then they try to sell them a pub crawl. A pub crawl means that a bus drives you around from bar to bar all night long. The main selling point of the pub crawl seems to be that you don't have to wait in lines to get into a bar. But there aren't really many lines to get into the bars of Waikīkī anyway.

Nor do the many glossy brochures that the Halekulani sends out in the mail mention that the horse drawn carriage for rent outside the hotel wears a sort of diaper contraption and some sort of rubber sheath over his penis. By the end of the night, the rubber sheath is full of urine. It also goes unmentioned in the brochure that the man who drives the carriage can often be seen emptying out the full sheath's bladder of urine on the street.

And the Halekulani's website does not mention that the Cellar, a bar that is famous for having a Chippendale's sort of night once a week, is right across the street. The Cellar uses the show as bait to bring in the girls (like everywhere, there is a constant girl shortage in Waikīkī's bars). And then after the show, the bouncers let the boys come in. The bouncers like to tell the boys that the girls are all ready for them after seeing the naked men. The bouncers at the Cellar sell underage drinkers a drink bracelet for $20. My roommate used to work the door at the Cellar. They used to give my

roommate a cut of this money each night.

The mai tai I get at the Halekulani when I finally get there comes with an orchid and a mint sprig and a piece of sugar cane over crushed ice. It is very sweet and strong and indigenous to California, not Hawai'i. I drink the mai tais in a bar with no windows. The waitresses wear long gray dresses, a sort of plantation-style outfit. Two men in tuxedos play standards. Despite the sign outside the bar that resort wear is required of all patrons after 6 pm, red faced tourists in t-shirts and shorts sit at various tables drinking.

six

I am fascinated with the constant disconnect between photographs of tourist locations in advertisements and the actual place, between guidebook descriptions and what you get.

Whenever I see an article about Waikīkī in travel magazines, I always make it a point to read it. They almost always mention the Halekulani. And if the article includes photographs of the Halekulani, the hotel looks stunning and isolated and quiet. Empty beach chairs glow in the twilight. The sun sets in the distance, behind an empty dinner table. The sides of the hotel shine in the late afternoon golden sun.

Guidebooks often mention that the earliest known radiocarbon settlement date for Waikīkī comes from the site of the Halekulani. To admit this is very cheeky of the Halekulani. It is not legal to build on important settlement sites.

The guidebooks also talk about the swaying kiawe and the hula that gets danced under it nightly by Kanoe Miller but none mention that kiawe, also known as mesquite, has been an unusually invasive and annoying tree because it desiccates an area by using all available water. It has lowered the water tables across the island.

And the guidebooks often talk about how the Halekulani is right on Gray's Beach (sometimes Grey's Beach). And they might mention that this beach is known for its healing waters. And that its Hawaiian name is Kawehewehe, which means the opening up (a reef here was opened up for a boat landing at some point).

In photos from the 1940s it does look like one could walk across the lawn of the Halekulani and onto the beach, although who knows if this beach was manufactured or not. Hotels in Waikīkī often build up their beaches with imported sand and have been doing this for some time.

Although the hotel is right on the water, what was Gray's Beach in the 1940s is now a sea wall.

The hotel has somehow managed to grow grass right up to the edge of their land. And then they've built a fence. And they've lined the fence with some sort of hedge that has long thorns. And then there is a raised walkway that is above the water instead of a sand beach. Chances are that the Halekulani built this wall because of shoreline retreat (because most of the beaches of Waikīkī are man made, they aren't very stable). But this hardening of the shoreline is another handy way for hotels to restrict access.

At one point there is a fenced bit of beach. This is right near the pool and this area is about four to five yards wide. The sea wall here is heavily trafficked. This beach is not very relaxing, not deserted, not private, not romantic, not clean.

To get to the beach from the Halekulani you have to pass

through several gates. And then walk through the walkway to the side steps to the beach. The walkway is often flooded ankle deep when the tide comes in and is filled with stagnant dirty water full of bandaids and paper cups and suntan lotion bottles.

The Halekulani's pamphlets claim "the reputation of Halekulani's oceanfront as one of the finest in Waikīkī."

It is also not true, as a sign claims, that only registered guests of the Halekulani are allowed into the Pacific ocean.

seven

Waikīkī is a weird and hard to figure out place.

There is the story of the Halekulani. Which is in part the story of how multinational corporations use colonial nostalgia to their advantage. The Halekulani claims to be "immortalized" in a Charlie Chan novel. Its website presents numerous photographs of old Hawai'i, including a photograph of Kanoe Miller dancing hula there in the 1960s. Most of their publicity glosses over the fact that the once family owned resort was bought in the 1980s by Mitsui Real Estate Development Co., Ltd. and the thirty-seven bungalows were replaced with five architecturally indistinct box-like towers.

The Halekulani is just one of a series of exclusive hotels that use colonial nostalgia to sell old Hawai'i to mainly Japanese tourists. The Sheraton Moana Surfrider is another one (their gimmick is a number of rocking chairs that overlook one of the busiest streets in

Waikīkī; I've never once seen anyone sitting in one). And the Royal
Hawaiian ("the pink palace of the Pacific," also Sheraton) is another.

And then there is the story of the Outrigger chain. The
Outriggers brought the working classes to Waikīkī (mainly working
class United States tourists; U.S. tourists with money tend to go to
Maui or Kauai). Most of its hotels are located a few blocks from the
beach. Most were built in the 1970s and are somewhat run down
now. The carpet is worn. The bed spreads are thin. The decor looks
like nothing has changed since it was built.

Some days I love this part of Waikīkī because it is so stupid, so
ugly, so impossible. It is the one place on O'ahu where there is
some urban street life. It is full of artificial color. One can get one's
photo taken with a bunch of birds from South America. A man
from Liverpool paints himself all in silver or gold and stands very
still for money. He has shared his craft with several others so now
there are often as many as three still, metallic men on a block.

There is a dog that has a pet mouse. Usually you can find someone playing an ukulele. Breakdancing lives on here as a thriving dance form.

But more often Waikīkī just makes me sad. I feel an empathy for the large amount of fellow working class midwesterners wandering around with fake smiles on their faces. I imagine these smiles as the result of having read guidebooks about Hawai'i and saved for years to replace if only for a week the awful midwestern rust and environmental decay with smooth sands, warm water, and tropical breezes only to wake up and find themselves broke and here, in the decaying urban jungle of Waikīkī.

eight

I tried to think some about public and private in this essay. But I could come up with nothing profound to say about it. It is obvious that private interests are always encroaching on public ones and that tourism just make this worse. Then tourism combined with colonialism is a lethal stew.

Public Access Shoreline Hawai'i vs. Hawai'i County Planning Commission, 1995 WL 515898 protects indigenous Hawaiians' traditional and customary rights of access to gather plants, harvest trees, and take game. In this decision the court said about the balance between the rights of private landowners and the rights of persons exercising traditional Hawaiian culture that "the western concept of exclusivity is not universally applicable in Hawai'i."

These rights, however, are constantly eroded by property owners who restrict physical access by fencing in areas, closing

roads, diverting water, not providing parking spaces, etc. A 1997 attempt by state legislators to regulate the law provoked large protests and was not passed. This was a victory.

But there is nothing really left to gather in Waikīkī. It is rare to see an endemic or indigenous plant. There are very few fish near its shores.

nine

There is nothing left to gather in Waikīkī because its story is a sort of fairy tale in reverse. Once upon a time it was a rich, thriving watershed. People came to the watershed and they appreciated its swamp land and its fresh water and they also appreciated its waves and its salt water and its corals and its fish. They built many loʻi (irrigated terraces) and loko iʻa (fishponds). The area was famous for the large amount of niu (coconut) planted there. Then an evil man named Dillingham came to the land. This man brought with him a demon, a dredge called Kewalo, which means the calling. The dredge called out to him day and night to use it. But there was no reason to dredge Waikīkī because the taro and the rice did so well. Because the fish did so well. Because the chickens that lived on the edges of the loʻi did so well. Because the niu did so well. Many people were happy at that time.

But the dredge Kewalo was not happy. And so the dredge called to Dillingham that a man had gotten yellow fever. This man probably got yellow fever in Mexico. But the dredge Kewalo told Dillingham to say that he got it from Waikīkī and that Waikīkī had to be dredged to prevent any more of the fever. Dillingham listened to the call and so did his friends and so the Ala Wai canal was created and the Kewalo dredged the canal and the fresh water all went into the canal and then into the ocean.

The dredge Kewalo was happy and Dillingham was happy that he listened to the song of the Kewalo because he got money to dredge the Ala Wai and then he got to keep the dirt and sell the dirt back to those who owned the drained wetlands and now needed the fill.

But the fresh water that went into the ocean was not happy. It was no longer filtered by the wetlands and it became full of silt and pesticides and oils and other urban run-off. It was so unhappy that it destroyed all the coral and then the fish died. The fresh water was

so unhappy that to this day in protest it constantly silts up. To this day, the Ala Wai requires dredging every ten years.

The Dillingham sort of thinking spread across the land. Because Waikīkī was once a wetland, it didn't have much of a beach and so sand was brought in to make a beach and this again silted the coral and again killed the fish. And things continued to die.

Now there are two sorts of people associated with Waikīkī. Those who sign deals in the spirit of the Kewalo and live the way of the dredge. That is most who have come to these islands from some place else. Our histories are too provisional and we do not know the stories before the dredge called out. It is hard for us to listen. And those who live the way of the watershed as much as they can. Some of these hear the call of the ghost of the dredge Kewalo and resist the way the water of the Ala Wai resists. Cline Kahue, for instance, has what his doctor calls an anti-caucasian psychosis. It causes him to push haoles into the Ala Wai. One day last year in June he pushed three of them into the Ala Wai. One died.

confession

I've only told a small story. There are layers on top of layers to this story. I am only beginning to understand them. My understanding of Waikīkī is only six years old and based on brief forays into the place. I have only skimmed the surface. And even though I now live right on the edge of it, I tend to drive through Waikīkī. I have not worked in Waikīkī , which is what I think it takes to really know it.

But Ida looked at my essay and she pointed out that I had left out the military. She is right. This is a long complicated story that requires pages of attention. I am nowhere smart enough to tell this story. But I should end by noting that, of course, Ft. DeRussy has the best beach on Waikīkī and on these beaches the military have special privileges.

—
121

PHOTOGRAPHS BY CANDACE AH NEE

N **37°** 46' 57" W **122°** 11' 8"

Gentle Now,
Don't Add to Heartache

one

We come into the world.
We come into the world and there it is.
The sun is there.
The brown of the river leading to the blue and the brown of the
ocean is there.
Salmon and eels are there moving between the brown and the
brown and the blue.
The green of the land is there.
Elders and youngers are there.
We come into the world and we are there.
Fighting and possibility and love are there.
And we begin to breathe.
We come into the world and there it is.
We come into the world without and we breathe it in.
We come into the world and begin to move between the brown and
the blue and the green of it.

two

We came into the world at the edge of a stream.
The stream had no name but it began from a spring and flowed
down a hill into the Scioto that then flowed into the Ohio that then
flowed into the Mississippi that then flowed into the Gulf of Mexico.

The stream was a part of us and we were a part of the stream and we
were thus part of the rivers and thus part of the gulfs and the oceans.
And we began to learn the stream.
We looked under stones for the caddisfly larvae and its adhesive.
We counted the creek chub and we counted the slenderhead darter.
We learned to recognize the large, upright, dense, candle-like
clusters of yellowish flowers at the branch ends of the horsechestnut
and we appreciated the feathery gracefulness of the drooping, but
upturning, branchlets of the larch.
We mimicked the catlike meow, the soft quirrt or kwut, and the
louder, grating ratchet calls of the gray catbird.
We put our heads together.
We put our heads together with all these things, with the caddisfly
larva, with the creek chub and the slenderhead darter, with the
horsechestnut and the larch, with the gray catbird.
We put our heads together on a narrow pillow, on a stone, on a
narrow stone pillow, and we talked to each other all day long
because we loved.
We loved the stream.
And we were of the stream.
And we couldn't help this love because we arrived at the bank of the
stream and began breathing and the stream was various and full of
information and it changed our bodies with its rotten with its cold
with its clean with its mucky with fallen leaves with its things that
bite the edges of the skin with its leaves with its sand and dirt with
its pungent at moments with its dry and prickly with its warmth with
its mushy and moist with its hard flat stones on the bottom with its

—

125

horizon lines of gently rolling hills with its darkness with its dappled light with its cicadas buzz with its trills of birds.

three

This is where we learned love and where we learned depth and where we learned layers and where we learned connections between layers.
We learned and we loved the black sandshell, the ash, the american bittern, the harelip sucker, the yellow bullhead, the beech, the great blue heron, the dobsonfly larva, the water penny larva, the birch, the redhead, the white catspaw, the elephant ear, the buckeye, the king eider, the river darter, the sauger, the burning bush, the common merganser, the limpet, the mayfly nymph, the cedar, the turkey vulture, the spectacle case, the flat floater, the cherry, the red tailed hawk, the longnose gar, the brook trout, the chestnut, the killdeer, the river snail, the giant floater, the chokeberry, gray catbird, the rabbitsfoot, the slenderhead darter, the crabapple, the american robin, the creek chub, the stonefly nymph, the dogwood, the warbling vireo, the sow bug, the elktoe, the elm, the marsh wren, the monkeyface, the central mudminnow, the fir, the gray-cheeked thrush, the white bass, the predaceous diving beetle, the hawthorn, the scud, the salamander mussel, the hazelnut, the warbler, the mapleleaf, the american eel, the hemlock, the speckled chub, the whirligig beetle larva, the hickory, the sparrow, the caddisfly

larva, the fluted shell, the horse chestnut, the wartyback, the white
heelsplitter, the larch, the pine grosbeak, the brook stickleback, the
river redhorse, the locust, the ebonyshelf, the giant water bug, the
maple, the eastern phoebe, the white sucker, the creek heelsplitter,
the mulberry, the crane fly larva, the mountain madtom, the oak,
the bank swallow, the wabash pigtoe, the damselfly larva, the
pine, the stonecat, the kidneyshell, the plum, the midge larva, the
eastern sand darter, the rose, the purple wartyback, the narrow-
winged damselfly, the spruce, the pirate perch, the threehorn
wartyback, the sumac, the black fly larva, the redside dace, the
tree-of-heaven, the orange-foot pimpleback, the dragonfly larva,
the walnut, the gold fish, the butterfly, the striped fly larva, the
willow, the freshwater drum, the ohio pigtoe, the warmouth, the
mayfly nymph, the clubshell.

And this was just the beginning of the list.

Our hearts took on many things.

Our hearts took on new shapes, new shapes every day as we went to
the stream every day.

Our hearts took on the shape of well-defined riffles and pools, clean
substrates, woody debris, meandering channels, floodplains, and
mature streamside forests.

Our hearts took on the shape of the stream and became riffled and
calmed and muddy and clean and flooded and shrunken dry.

Our hearts took on the shape of whirligigs swirling across the water.

We shaped our hearts into the sycamore trees along the side of the
stream and we let into our hearts the long pendulous polygamous
racemes of its small green flowers, the first-formed male flowers

—

127

with no pistil and then the later arriving hairy ovary with its two curved stigmas.

We let ourselves love the one day of the adult life of the mayfly as it swarms, mates in flight, and dies all without eating.

And we shaped our hearts into the water willow and into the eggs spawned in the water willow.

Our hearts took on the brilliant blues, reds, and oranges of breeding male rainbow darter and our hearts swam to the female rainbow darter and we poked her side with our snout as she buried herself under the gravel and we laid upon her as she vibrated.

We let leaves and algae into our hearts and then we let the mollusks and the insects and we let the midge larvae into our heart and then the stonefly nymph and then a minnow came into our heart and with it a bass and then we let the blue heron fly in, the raccoon amble by, the snapping turtle and the watersnake also.

We immersed ourselves in the shallow stream. We lied down on the rocks on our narrow pillow stone and let the water pass over us and our heart was bathed in glochida and other things that attach to the flesh.

And as we did this we sang.

We sang gentle now.

Gentle now clubshell,

don't add to heartache.

Gentle now warmouth, mayfly nymph,

don't add to heartache.

Gentle now willow, freshwater drum, ohio pigtoe,

don't add to heartache.

Gentle now walnut, gold fish, butterfly, striped fly larva,
don't add to heartache.
Gentle now black fly larva, redside dace, tree-of-heaven, orange-
foot pimpleback, dragonfly larva,
don't add to heartache.
Gentle now purple wartyback, narrow-winged damselfly, spruce,
pirate perch, threehorn wartyback, sumac,
don't add to heartache.
Gentle now pine, stonecat, kidneyshell, plum, midge larva, eastern
sand darter, rose,
don't add to heartache.
Gentle now creek heelsplitter, mulberry, crane fly larva, mountain
madtom, oak, bank swallow, wabash pigtoe, damselfly larva,
don't add to heartache.
Gentle now pine grosbeak, brook stickleback, river redhorse, locust,
ebonyshelf, giant water bug, maple, eastern phoebe, white sucker,
don't add to heartache.
Gentle now whirligig beetle larva, hickory, sparrow, caddisfly larva,
fluted shell, horse chestnut, wartyback, white heelsplitter, larch,
don't add to heartache.
Gentle now white bass, predaceous diving beetle, hawthorn, scud,
salamander mussel, hazelnut, warbler, mapleleaf, american eel,
hemlock, speckled chub,
don't add to heartache.
Gentle now stonefly nympth, dogwood, warbling vireo, sow bug,
elktoe, elm, marsh wren, monkeyface, central mudminnow, fir,
gray-cheeked thrush,

don't add to heartache.

Gentle now longnose gar, brook trout, chestnut, killdeer, river snail, giant floater, chokeberry, gray catbird, rabbitsfoot, slenderhead darter, crabapple, american robin, creek chub,

don't add to heartache.

Gentle now king eider, river darter, sauger, burning bush, common merganser, limpet, mayfly nymph, cedar, turkey vulture, spectacle case, flat floater, cherry, red tailed hawk,

don't add to heartache.

Gentle now black sandshell, ash, american bittern, harelip sucker, yellow bullhead, beech, great blue heron, dobsonfly larva, water penny larva, birch, redhead, white catspaw, elephant ear, buckeye,

don't add to heartache.

Gentle now, we sang,

Circle our heart in rapture, in love-ache. Circle our heart.

four

It was not all long lines of connection and utopia.

It was a brackish stream and it went through the field beside our house.

But we let into our hearts the brackish parts of it also.

Some of it knowingly.

We let in soda cans and we let in cigarette butts and we let in pink tampon applicators and we let in six pack of beer connectors and

we let in various other pieces of plastic that would travel through
the stream.

And some of it unknowingly.

We let the run off from agriculture, surface mines, forestry, home
wastewater treatment systems, construction sites, urban yards,
and roadways into our hearts.

We let chloride, magnesium, sulfate, manganese, iron, nitrite/
nitrate, aluminum, suspended solids, zinc, phosphorus, fertilizers,
animal wastes, oil, grease, dioxins, heavy metals and lead go
through our skin and into our tissues.

We were born at the beginning of these things, at the time of
chemicals combining, at the time of stream run off.

These things were a part of us and would become more a part of us
but we did not know it yet.

Still we noticed enough to sing a lament.

To sing in lament for whoever lost her elephant ear lost her
mountain madtom

and whoever lost her butterfly lost her harelip sucker

and whoever lost her white catspaw lost her rabbitsfoot

and whoever lost her monkeyface lost her speckled chub

and whoever lost her wartyback lost her ebonyshell

and whoever lost her pirate perch lost her ohio pigtoe lost her
clubshell.

five

What I did not know as I sang the lament of what was becoming lost
and what was already lost was how this loss would happen.
I did not know that I would turn from the stream to each other.
I did not know I would turn to each other.
That I would turn to each other to admire the softness of each
other's breast, the folds of each other's elbows, the brightness
of each other's eyes, the smoothness of each other's hair, the
evenness of each other's teeth, the firm blush of each other's lips,
the firm softness of each other's breasts, the fuzz of each other's
down, the rich, ripe pungency of each other's smell, all of it, each
other's cheeks, legs, neck, roof of mouth, webbing between the
fingers, tips of nails and also cuticles, hair on toes, whorls on
fingers, skin discolorations.
I turned to each other.
Ensnared, bewildered, I turned to each other and from the stream.
I turned to each other and I began to work for the chemical
factory and I began to work for the paper mill and I began to work
for the atomic waste disposal plant and I began to work at
keeping men in jail.
I turned to each other.
I didn't even say goodbye elephant ear, mountain madtorn, butterfly,
harelip sucker, white catspaw, rabbitsfoot, monkeyface, speckled
chub, wartyback, ebonyshell, pirate perch, ohio pigtoe, clubshell.
I replaced what I knew of the stream with Lifestream Total
Cholesterol Test Packets, with Snuggle Emerald Stream Fabric
Softener Dryer Sheets, with Tisserand Aromatherapy Aroma-

Stream Cartridges, with Filter Stream Dust Tamer, and Streamzap PC
Remote Control, Acid Stream Launcher, and Viral Data Stream.
I didn't even say goodbye elephant ear, mountain madtorn, butterfly,
harelip sucker, white catspaw, rabbitsfoot, monkeyface, speckled
chub, wartyback, ebonyshell, pirate perch, ohio pigtoe, clubshell.
I put a Streamline Tilt Mirror in my shower and I kept a crystal
Serenity Sphere with a Winter Stream view on my dresser.
I didn't even say goodbye elephant ear, mountain madtorn, butterfly,
harelip sucker, white catspaw, rabbitsfoot, monkeyface, speckled
chub, wartyback, ebonyshell, pirate perch, ohio pigtoe, clubshell.

I bought a Gulf Stream Blue Polyester Boat Cover for my 14-16 Foot
V-Hull Fishing boat with beam widths up to sixty-eight feet and I
talked about value stream management with men in suits over a desk.
I didn't even say goodbye elephant ear, mountain madtorn, butterfly,
harelip sucker, white catspaw, rabbitsfoot, monkeyface, speckled
chub, wartyback, ebonyshell, pirate perch, ohio pigtoe, clubshell.
I just turned to each other and the body parts of the other suddenly
glowed with the beauty and detail that I had found in the stream.
I put my head together on a narrow pillow and talked with each other
all night long.
And I did not sing.
I did not sing otototoi; dark, all merged together, oi.
I did not sing groaning words.
I did not sing otototoi; dark, all merged together, oi.
I did not sing groaning words.
I did not sing o wo, wo, wo!
I did not sing I see, I see.
I did not sing wo, wo!

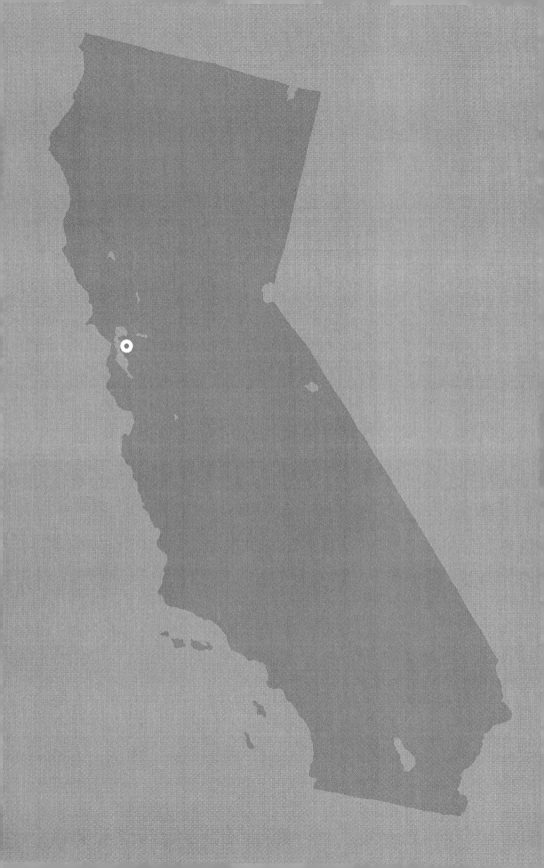

N **37°** 51' 49" W **122°** 15' 58"

The Incinerator

one

We are at the incinerator behind the house. It is a four foot square
made out of cinderblocks, about three feet high. I have just
dumped our trash in there and then set it on fire

then set it on fire. We are now sitting on the edge, away from the
smoke, striking matches against the cinderblocks. When they
flare we hold onto them until they burn our fingers

until they burn our fingers and then we throw them into the
incinerator. I drop one of the matches on my leg, faking injury
so as to lean into Chillicothe. Chillicothe leans back. We turn
towards each other

turn towards each other and as if we did it all the time, I start
unbuttoning Chillicothe's shirt. It is difficult to unbutton because
it has many small white buttons and as I do it I keep fumbling

as I do it I keep fumbling. Chillicothe seems disconnected from
what's happening. I pull the shirt open, exposing the roads we
take through hilltops and hollows, as we travel the line between
glaciated and the unglaciated and I look down at Chillicothe,
grinning, unable to believe I am actually about to do

unable to believe I am actually about to do what I have dreamed of
so many times, and then Chillicothe says, "This is my first time."
I laugh. I say, "You're kidding." Chillicothe whispers back, "I'm
sorry." I look down at Chillicothe, my grin fading, marveling at
flatness giving way to rolling hills

flatness giving way to rolling hills. Chillicothe lies beneath me,
embarrassed and vulnerable. This is not the mythically carnal
creature of my fantasies; this is a nervous child. Chillicothe says

"I still want to do it... I just thought I should tell you... in case you
     wondered why I wasn't... better."
why I wasn't... better." And then over the Scioto, the Big Scioto, the
     Great Scioto, a fine river, yet also just one among many, and yet
     still the one that carved the valley, this valley exceptionally wide.
this valley exceptionally wide as I am fucking with Chillicothe in the
     vegetable garden behind the house. No one can see us because
     we are lying down in between the rows of corn. I am atop
     Chillicothe and I straddle Chillicothe's chest. My breasts are in
     Chillicothe's face and Chillicothe cups them
and Chillicothe cups them amid floodplain soils and the hills that
     extend south past the farm lands and their ordered squares
     as I lean down and stick my tongue in Chillicothe's mouth. I
     kiss Chillicothe, move Chillicothe's hands up, hold both of
     Chillicothe's arms above Chillicothe's head. Then my hips are
     above Chillicothe's face now,
hips above Chillicothe's face, moving slightly, oh-so slightly. And
     then out of the valley, past Mt Pisgah and Swiger Knob, the wild
     game trails, the war trails, I lower my hips onto Chillicothe's
     face, then lower over chest, navel. Then my hands are inside
my hands are inside going south to Portsmouth, to the river, and
     then on south to Ashland, and Chillicothe's head arches back,
     throat white as I also arch back, hips grind, breasts high.
hips grind, breasts high and somewhere along the way the
     hills meet the sky evenly and the air gets so heavy it is often
     called blue.

two

1969, 17.8 percent poverty in Appalachia.

1979, 14.1 percent.

And not really rooted in economics.

And sometimes when people came by the radio station she would
curse at them and tell them that my father was a son of a bitch.

And the apartment buildings to the right of our house.

And then the map was the world.

Appalachia had forty jobs per 100 people in 1969.

As I write this other stories keep popping up and I keep abandoning
them: the nuances around race in the contemporary US.

As I write this other stories keep popping up and I keep abandoning
them: she was probably saying something about how she did
not see her life in the static and unhappy way working class
lives were presented in books and movies.

As I write this other stories keep popping up and I keep abandoning
them: shame about being working class transformed into
claims of authenticity from her generation to my generation.

As I write this other stories keep popping up and I keep abandoning
them: class has something relational about it, making its
discussion in the US, one of the wealthiest countries in the
world, especially fraught.

As I write this other stories keep popping up and I keep abandoning
them: the hours I spent drinking beers with the baggers in
grocery store parking lots.

As I write this other stories keep popping up and I keep abandoning

them: the intense humidity and haze of summer that defines
   the region with its own beauty.
As I write this other stories keep popping up and I keep abandoning
   them: the feeling of obligation to fuck the men who worked at
   the papermill because they worked at the papermill.
As I write this other stories keep popping up and I keep abandoning
   them: the alphabetical list as a device that falsely suggests
   there might be a place for everything.
But if I pulled the shade, I was worried that my father might get
   fired.
He did a 4 am shift on the air and then once that was done at 10 am
   he would sell advertisements until evening.
Huge piles of wood chips.
I also knew she was upper class because she could look out a
   window in her house and see into the radio station through the
   bathroom window.
I am wondering what calling myself working class covers over.
I assume people who identified as other races lived there also but I
   don't know the names of those races because at the time I only
   saw black and white.
I had grown up by defining class as being about the sort of housing
   one had in relation to one's neighbors.
I meant to tell a story of privilege.
I remember loud machines.
I started working at the radio station when I was sixteen.
I was not by any means the only one.
I was worried that the boss might look at me in the bathroom.

If someone closed the bathroom door, she would get on the phone
and call over and tell them to open it.

In 1960 the region had 6.8 percent unemployment and the nation
had 5 percent.

In 1969 per capita income was 78 percent of the rest of the nation's.

It was illegal at the time to rent only to white people without
children.

It was owned by his boss and was a short walk from the radio
station where he worked.

My parents had lived there when they first moved to Chillicothe.

Not only did she live in a house but she lived in a fancy house.

On school trips we went each year to visit the paper mill.

Population only grew 1 percent that decade, while the nation grew
20 percent.

Right after my birthday.

She also owned the house we lived in.

She did this often and if she saw someone goofing around she
would get on the phone and call over to the radio station and tell
them to get back to work.

Some big and dusty.

Some smelling like fermentation.

The 1964 report noted that Appalachia lost 2 million people due to
migration between 1950 and 1960.

The 1970 census revealed that 18 percent had incomes below the
official poverty level.

The 1970s was a pivotal decade because the region relied heavily on
coal mining and the OPEC oil embargo contributed to a global

increase in the price of coal.

The anxiety in her voice when the car needed repair.

The buildings to the left were also owned by my father's boss and
she only rented to white people without children.

The buildings to the right were rented to black and white people
with and without children.

The computer had three wheels and the wheels held cartridges that
had the local advertisements and weather and news on them.

The corporation, we called it Quigg, after the man who was our
contact with it, fired Cherokee Maiden and the Secret Squirrel
and replaced them with a computer.

The house was located between two sets of apartment buildings.

The map was the neighborhood.

The upper class boss was gone and replaced by a corporation.

The upper class boss would fire my father all the time but it never
stuck.

The visits started with trips to the factory floor.

The war on poverty was declared for Appalachia in 1964.

There was one in three in poverty.

There was the idea that a rising tide lifts all boats.

There were other signs of our being middle class, or so I was told.

This was the sort of thing that upper class people did.

We bought our food without food stamps and we talked about how
we did this a lot as a point of pride and distinction.

We lived in a country that was rich and the government had given
the place where we lived a lot of aid starting in 1964 to pull it out
of poverty.

We worried a lot about my father getting fired.

What calling myself middle class covers over.

What I remember most about these factory tours were the piles of
    materials.

What it opens up.

What it opens up.

When I was growing up, the owner of the radio station was upper
    class.

When I went to the radio station, I was too nervous to go to the
    bathroom.

three

I was trying to understand my mother when she called us middle
    class all through my childhood. And why she said this since by
    all the markers of economic resources, education, and cultural
    access within the US we were working class. When I years later
    asked her why, she said that we were middle class because we
    lived in a house between two apartment buildings.

I was trying to think about what was right about what she said.

The house she was talking about was owned by my father's
    boss. It was built out of cinderblocks and it had four rooms
    plus a bathroom: a kitchen and a living room at the front;
    two bedrooms at the back. It also had a carport and a gravel
    driveway leading to the carport. It had a linoleum floor. It had
    two picture windows, one looked out on the carport and one on
    the apartments next door. The house was pleasant. Its main

drawback was that it leaked a lot and was very damp so things
in the house tended to get covered with a green mildew if left on
the floor.

When my mother was saying we were middle class she was saying
something less about our house and more about our location on
the block and about our location on the globe at the same time.

I was trying to think about what was right about what she said.

I was trying to think about the role of the US government in forcing
reduced tariff barriers on numerous countries.

I was trying to think about the General Agreement on Tariffs
and Trade.

I was trying to think about women packing ice cream in the
Gaza Strip.

I was trying to think about the World Trade Organization.

I was trying to think about women sewing garments in Liberia.

I was trying to think about the North American Free Trade
Agreement.

I was trying to think about women shelling shrimp in Honduras.

I was trying to think about the Dominican Republic-Central America
Free Trade Agreement.

I was trying to think about women cultivating cassava in Zambia.

I was trying to think about a number of bilateral agreements.

I was trying to think about women panning the tailings of diamond
gravel for gold in Sierra Leone.

I was trying to think about Hannah Weiner's "Radcliffe and
Guatemalan Women."

Weiner keeps one eye on herself, one eye on her neighborhood

and one eye on another place as she puts statements about
Radcliffe women and Guatemalan women side by side. It is not
known when Weiner wrote "Radcliffe and Guatemalan Women"
but she probably wrote it in the 1980s.

She might have been thinking about how the 1980s began in
    Guatemala with the police burning alive thirty-nine people
    who were occupying or were hostages of those occupying the
    Spanish Embassy.

She might have been thinking about how the intensity of
    government killings peaked in 1982, with estimates of at least
    18,000 state killings in that year alone.

She might have been thinking about the scorched earth campaign
    that in addition to killing hundreds of thousands displaced
    about one million people.

She might have been thinking about how the decade ended, in
    August and September of 1989, with the government kidnapping
    and then "disappearing" a number of student leaders.

She might have been thinking about how the Guatemalan
    government did all of this with the support of the US
    government.

She might have been thinking about how the US government began
    funding the security forces of the Guatemalan government
    in the 1960s and how close ties remained between the two
    governments through the 1980s.

"Radcliffe and Guatemalan Women" is probably all found language
    but I do not know this for sure. The sentences that are obviously
    about Radcliffe women sound as if they are from an alumna

—

145

magazine. Some of the sentences that are obviously about Guatemalan women are from Severo Martínez Peláez's La patria del criollo, a book not yet translated into English; others seem to be from some sort of human rights report.

Weiner's piece is full of juxtaposition, fragmentation, and lack of attribution as if to suggest that there is nothing easy to say about this relationship between Radcliffe women and Guatemalan women. She avoids presenting herself as a knowing but uninvolved witness, as the clichéd poet-prophet. And as Weiner was a Radcliffe graduate, the piece also suggests that she might be a participant and part of the problem.

But at the same time, even while the categories "Radcliffe women" and "Guatemalan women" are not equal—one is a group of women from a university and one is a group of women from a nation—the piece also suggests that there is a relationship, a complicated relationship between the two categories. This relationship is the multi-eyed aspect of "Radcliffe and Guatemalan Women."

"Radcliffe and Guatemalan Women" makes me profoundly uneasy.

It makes me uneasy that the Radcliffe women and the Guatemalan women are presumed opposites, one privileged and one not.

It makes me uneasy that at the same time the Radcliffe women and the Guatemalan women are a specific sort of joined opposites, joined by their gender, by the ties that their governments have with each other, and by the ties that they have with their governments.

It makes me uneasy that Weiner more or less treats both categories
of women equally; neither the Radcliffe women nor the
Guatemalan women have any depth. While there are some
names mentioned in the piece, they are not really present as
individuals in the poem and it is often not clear which sentences
are about Guatemalan women and which sentences are about
Radcliffe women.

It makes me uneasy that as nothing is attributed, I cannot stop
myself from guessing at whether it was a Radcliffe or a
Guatemalan woman who "had to raise five children by herself."
But the minute I guess, I have to think again and wonder
about the relationship between guess and cliché and cultural
assumptions.

It makes me uneasy that Weiner frequently includes statements
that would be true about both Radcliffe and Guatemalan women,
such as "They are paid lower wages than the men," as if these
lower wages are in any way equivalent.

While thinking about my mother's assertion that we were middle
class, while thinking about "Radcliffe and Guatemalan Women,"
while thinking about women's employment in the countries
with the highest percentage of women in poverty, while
thinking about how the manipulation of trade barriers by the
US government has adversely impacted women across many
different nations, while thinking about how at the same time
the global economy empowers some women and disempowers
others, I was trying to think about what sort of vision one
needed to have in order to keep one eye on the neighborhood

and then one eye on the nation and then yet one more eye
on the world.

I was trying to think, in other words.

I wanted to write something about Chillicothe. I am from Chillicothe.
In my family, I was the Chillicothian. My parents were from
somewhere else. And yet I am not really a Chillicothian anymore
and that feels obvious when I go back there. So my next thought
was then, oh maybe it is that I am a child of Chillicothe. And I sat
down to figure out what that might mean. I was trying to write
something about being a child of a certain moment, of a certain
class, working class, and then an adult of a different moment, of
a different class, middle class.

I was attempting to grow some other eyes. I wanted to write
something about Chillicothe, even as my story is not the story
of Chillicothe, even as Chillicothe and I both benefit from the
economic incentives that Lyndon B. Johnson's 1964 war on
poverty allocates to Appalachia, even as I take these incentives
and I leave town and benefit from globalization in numerous
ways, even as I continue to benefit today, even as Chillicothe's
fortunes dwindle a few years after NAFTA when its industries go
south.

Each morning, as I tried to develop a multi-eyed focus, I would sit
down at my desk and go into a trance and write down whatever
came up. I left Chillicothe more or less for good when I was
twenty-one so I ended up with a lot of childhood memories.
Most of them personally pleasant. I kept these totems in a file
and when I got tired of gathering them, I would try to rebuild

the town from the outside, from statistics, and I would arrange all
these parts of Chillicothe in various patterns and try to see what
sort of place the various patterns made.

four

When I went to college this house where I grew up became lower
middle class.
We never talked about class at college.
We didn't talk much about class in graduate school either.
Unemployment for Appalachia fluctuated over the period, with the
unemployment rate in 2000 at 5.7 percent higher than the 1970
rate of 4.0 percent.
Three to one gap in incomes between the richest and poorest
countries in 1820.
Thirty-five to one gap in 1950.
They worried me.
Then it continued with a teaching assistant line in graduate school.
Then I realized something about education and class mobility.
Then I kept this definition but moved from block to nation.
Then I did as told and got a scholarship.
Then I also began to think about how I lived in one of the richest
countries in the world.
The per capita income of Chillicothe was $19,101 in 2000.
That one could say one was Appalachian and more or less mean that
one was lower class.
So I was able to deduce then that I was not middle class.

So at the same moment that a book told me that I could think of
   myself as marginal or at risk or disadvantaged, I also realized
   that I was reading a book that I had access to because I was no
   longer Appalachian because this book was not sold in my town.
Seventy-two to one gap in incomes between the richest and poorest
   countries in 1992.

Once I did this, I realized I lived in Appalachia.
No one told me this.
Most of my fellow PhDs had to quit looking for academic work after
   an unsuccessful first year and get other sorts of jobs and then
   the jobs they got didn't give them time necessary to look for
   academic work.
Mine began with a scholarship.
In each category, it lagged the nation by more than 30 percentage
   points.
In 1999, 13.7 percent people in poverty in Appalachia.
In 1989, 15.4 percent people in poverty.
I was able to go to graduate school because the university wanted
   some cheap labor.
I thought I was getting something for free from the university but
   really they were giving me a minimum wage job and calling it a
   mentorship and a scholarship.
I should have figured it out then.
I do remember my high school guidance counselor telling me
   to apply to rich private schools because these schools
   were interested in diversity and would give Appalachians
   scholarships; she was talking about how white women were

beneficiaries of affirmative action although she didn't say it
that way.

I attended graduate school with a number of others from working
classes.

Forty-four to one gap in incomes between the richest and poorest
countries in 1973.

For if we were middle class on the block, and lower class in the
nation, we were upper class in the world, or in other words, the
terms were so relationally slippery they were hard to define.

Eleven to one gap in 1913.

Can you see where I started to get stuck?

By 1992 per capita income for Appalachia had reached 83 percent.

But the whole time I was growing up, no one once told me I was
Appalachian.

But no, it took me buying a book on Appalachia and looking at the
little map in the book to realize that Appalachia included the
southern part of Ohio where I was from.

Between 1992 and today, my salary doubles.

Between 1989 and 1992, my salary quadruples.

Between 1970 and 2000, the poverty rate in Appalachia dropped
from 17.8 percent to 13.7 percent.

Before graduate school it had been a home.

At that moment I began to think that maybe my mother was
underestimating when she kept insisting we were middle class.

As I write this other stories keep popping up and I keep
abandoning them: wanting to talk about class, I kept talking
only about gender.

As I write this other stories keep popping up and I keep
abandoning them: when I sat down to write this piece I began
by writing about myself using a series statements that I stole
from working class memoirs by US women and then memoirs
by women from the global south.

As I write this other stories keep popping up and I keep
abandoning them: the categories were not equal: working
class US women and then just any woman from the global
south, as if these categories had any relationship between
them.

As I write this other stories keep popping up and I keep
abandoning them: education's complicated relationship to
class.

As I write this other stories keep popping up and I keep
abandoning them: alternative ways of living one's life, the
alternative ways of seeing things that can at moments be
induced by drug use that was such a part of Weiner.

As I write this other stories keep popping up and I keep
abandoning them: the difficulty of categorizing Weiner,
Radcliffe graduate then lingerie model then tuned in and
dropped out language poet who sees words on people's heads.

As I write this other stories keep popping up and I keep
abandoning them: the participation by elite US universities in
US foreign policy.

As I write this other stories keep popping up and I keep
abandoning them: it makes me more nervous to put sentences
about myself next to sentences about women from other

places than it would to put sentences about myself next to sentences that are about men and women from other places.

As I write this other stories keep popping up and I keep abandoning them: in terms of unemployment, the numbers for Appalachia today more closely resemble those of the rest of the nation but at the same time are still not that different from the numbers that so defined the region in 1964 when it was exemplary of poverty.

As I write this other stories keep popping up and I keep abandoning them: my current income puts me in one of the top income percentiles of the world yet I continue to think of myself as broke.

As I write this other stories keep popping up and I keep abandoning them: I wanted to end this piece with a scene of metaphoric group sex where all the participants were place names, but the minute I attempted to do this I got bogged down in questions of which places would penetrate and which places would be penetrated.

five

epilogue

These are the roads we take

      the roads we take through

hilltops and hollows,

standing at the line

        the line that distinguishes the glaciated

from the unglaciated marveling

          marveling at the flatness giving way

            flatness giving way to

   rolling hills.

Over the Scioto,

    the Big Scioto,

    the Great Scioto,

a fine river

and yet also one among many,

      one among many and yet still

the one that carved the valley,

      carved this valley, exceptionally wide,

         exceptionally wide as it left

floodplain soils amid the hills that extend south

         extend south

past the farm lands with their ordered squares

and out of the valley, past Mt Pisgah and Swiger Knob.

      past Mt Pisgah and Swiger Knob,

the wild game trails,

the war trails,

south to Portsmouth, to the river,

                  to the river, south to Ashland

somewhere along the way

the hills meet the sky

        meet the sky evenly,

the air gets heavy.

It is often called blue.

    Often called blue,

it is all there,

the black sandstone,

the dissected plateaus,

eroded and rough,

       and rough,

layers of limestone,

sandstone,

shale,

and coal sediment.

Streams going off in all directions.

       Going off in all directions,

the road, almost cultureless,

exits at even intervals, floats

             floats above

above the desire I want

      the desire I want as epilogue,

            as epilogue, for in my heart seeds

                 heart seeds of

  unending love,

      love, still, and also despite.

—

155